Table of Contents

TABLE OF CONTENTS 3

INTRODUCTION 10

CHAPTER 1: HOW HIGH CAN YOU GO? 15

    MAKING PROFIT 15

    THE DEMAND 18

    BE REALISTIC 19

CHAPTER 2: LET'S TALK ABOUT MONEY 21

    COST GET STARTED 22

    HIDDEN COSTS 26

    KNOW THE NUMBERS 26

    GETTING THE BEST FINANCING 30

    HOME EQUITY LOANS/LINES OF CREDIT 36

    ALTERNATIVE FINANCING OPTIONS 37

    CONTRACT FLIPPING 43

CHAPTER 3: GETTING STARTED 45

    DECIDE ON WHAT YOU WANT 45

    SINGLE OR MULTIFAMILY UNITS 46

    MAKING A PLAN 48

    TYPES OF RENTAL PROPERTY 55

Rental Property 59

Mobile Homes 61

Commercial 62

Foreclosures 63

Setting Up Bank Accounts 65

CHAPTER 4: WHERE TO FIND PROPERTY 69

Finding Property 69

Choosing the Right Property 74

The Short Sale 85

CHAPTER 5: BUYING THE PROPERTY 89

Step 1 Escrow 90

Step 2 Title Search 90

Step 3 Find an Attorney 92

Step 4 Get Pre-Approved for a Mortgage 94

Step 5 Negotiate Closing Costs 95

Step 6 Home Inspection 96

Step 7 Pest Inspection 97

Step 8 Renegotiate 97

Step 9 Lock in the Interest Rate 100

Step 10 - Deal with Contingencies 103

Step 11 Fund Escrow 104

Step 12 Final Walkthrough 105

Real Estate Investing Rental Property:

Complete Beginner's Guide on how to Buy, Rehab and Manage Apartments to build up remarkable Passive Income and reach Financial Freedom even with no money down

By

Brandon Hammond

Step 13 Sign the Papers 105

CHAPTER 6: SHOULD I REHAB? 108

Consider the Costs 108

Time 111

Money 113

Practicality 115

Finding a Contractor 121

Do You Need a Subcontractor? 124

Ugly is Beautiful 126

CHAPTER 7: MANAGING THE PROPERTY 128

Should You Hire a Manager? 129

Paying Your Property Manager 135

Investment of Time 137

Renting Out Your Property 138

Pricing Your Property 141

Showing the Property 142

Pets or No Pets 144

Writing the Lease 146

The Search for a Property Manager 147

CHAPTER 8: RISKS AND MYTHS 151

Risk #1: Unpredictable Market 152

Risk #2: Be Location Conscious 153

Risk #3: Negative Cash Flow 154

Risk #4: Vacancy Risk 155

Risk #5: Bad Tenants 156

Risk #6: Hidden Property Damage 156

Risk #7: Lack of Liquidity 157

Risk #8: Foreclosure 157

Risk #9: Depreciation 158

Risk #10: Vacation Rental Issues 158

Common Myths on Real Estate Investing 159

CHAPTER 9: COMMON MISTAKES FOR NEW INVESTORS 164

Failing Research 165

Hesitation 166

Failing to Look at Enough Properties 168

Getting Too Emotionally Involved 170

Real Estate is a Get Rich Quick Scheme 172

Ignoring the Fine Print 173

CONCLUSION 177

© Copyright 2018 by __Brandon Hammond__ - All rights reserved.

The following eBook is reproduced below with the goal of providing information that is as accurate and reliable as possible. Regardless, purchasing this eBook can be seen as consent to the fact that both the publisher and the author of this book are in no way experts on the topics discussed within and that any recommendations or suggestions that are made herein are for entertainment purposes only. Professionals should be consulted as needed prior to undertaking any of the action endorsed herein.

This declaration is deemed fair and valid by both the American Bar Association and the Committee of Publishers Association and is legally binding throughout the United States.

Furthermore, the transmission, duplication, or reproduction of any of the following work including specific information will be considered an illegal act irrespective of if it is done electronically or in print. This extends to creating a secondary or tertiary copy of the work or a recorded copy and is only allowed with the express written consent from the Publisher. All additional rights reserved.

The information in the following pages is broadly considered a truthful and accurate account of facts and as such, any inattention, use, or misuse of the information in question by the reader will render any resulting actions solely under their purview. There are no scenarios in which the publisher or the original author of this work can be in any fashion deemed liable for any hardship or damages that may befall them after undertaking information described herein.

Additionally, the information in the following pages is intended only for informational purposes and should thus be thought of as universal. As befitting its nature, it is presented without assurance regarding its prolonged validity or interim quality. Trademarks that are mentioned are done without written consent and can in no way be considered an endorsement from the trademark holder.

Introduction

Congratulations on downloading *Real Estate Investing* and thank you for doing so.

It is not just the American dream, but it is the dream of people all over the world to grasp the ability to own their own home. It's at the core of every person's soul. It is why they work for years in a job, so that they can pay the mortgage all the way to the end when they can finally say, "It's all mine." Yes, owning property is more than acquiring a possession, it is a reflection of status, success, and worthiness in a society that is entirely driven by money. But there are many more reasons why investing in real estate is a good idea; some you may have never thought of.

Historically, real estate has offered a much lower risk than any other investment opportunity. In most cases, once you have purchased the property, simply holding onto it can increase your wealth. Unlike paying rent every month, when you pay your mortgage you are in effect, paying yourself. If in the future, you try to sell, you will be able to reap all those mortgage payments back and more. The longer you hold onto the property, the more worth it has to you.

Compared to the stock market, where many things that can affect your wealth are completely out of your control, in real estate, the risk never changes. Because it is a tangible asset that can be leveraged to create different revenue streams, you have an almost foolproof investment tool you can rely on.

As long as you own real estate you have something with value. Whether it is land, or an office building, an apartment building, or just your personal home, your property is a real, tangible asset. It is something you can touch and can reasonably expect to increase in value over time. Unlike stocks you may own, your property is the type of asset that can be defended and protected even during disastrous situations.

There are many investment tools you can put your money in, but real estate is the only one that consistently withstood the test of time. No matter what the economic situation may be, the housing market has always recovered from whatever hits it. Values may decline for a time, but they always bounce back and eventually appreciate.

Without a doubt, a significant number of opportunities await you when you choose to make real estate your primary investment tool and this book is going to teach you how to take advantage of them. In the following pages you're going to learn:

- Just how much you can make in the real estate market
- How to decide which type of real estate investing is best for you
- How to get started
- How to make a solid real estate plan
- How to find the right property
- How to take a beast and turn it into a beauty
- How to avoid many of the mistakes new investors get into
- How to turn a small investment into a huge profit
- And so much more

When you invest in real estate, you're not only investing in one of the safest instruments available, but you can also turn that investment into a passive income that will provide you with years of stress-free life to carry you through your retirement years. Yes, you can build your own personal empire with real estate, and we're going to show you how to get started right now.

Welcome to a world of financial freedom and security in real estate. Now, let's get started.

There are plenty of books on this subject on the market, so thanks again for choosing this one! Every effort was made to ensure it is full of as much useful information as possible, please enjoy!

Chapter 1: How High Can You Go?

It's no secret that there is a lot of money to be made in real estate. Even a layperson understands that any reasonably priced property can generate revenue. Many who have purchased a single-family home and held onto it until the mortgage was paid off, can attest to the increase in value and the huge amount of equity it built up over the years. The reward is far more than what they would have received if they had placed the money in a savings account. Savings accounts only increase in worth when you decide to use the property to generate rental income.

Making Profit

There are many ways to make money with real estate. The simplest way is to buy the property and on hold it. As long as you maintain the property well, it will appreciate in value over time. Each time you make a payment, you build up equity in the property. When you sell it, you get all the equity you put into it back plus the appreciation.

Of course, the method above is the easiest way to make money in real estate, but if you apply other strategies, you can increase that profit potential exponentially. For example, you can use the property to generate rental income, you can invest in commercial property, you can take advantage of the tax breaks offered, and you can increase value by making improvements, and so on.

When it comes to making money in real estate, the sky is the limit. How much money you make will depend on how creative you are with your property and what you decide to do with it. The more you know about the rental market and how to capitalize on its benefits the higher potential return on your investment. There have been people who have lost every dime they had hoped to earn and then some in real estate investing, but they have also been those who have amassed millions of dollars on the same venture.

Investing in real estate is very much like anything else. You can fail or succeed based on how prepared you are before you begin. If you are serious about going down the rental route, then know that there is much more involved than just buying property, putting some tenants in there and collecting rent. You also need to be concerned with location, type of unit you are buying, the condition of the property, cost of maintenance, and a host of other details you'll have to address before you can even start getting your first tenant.

The same thing applies to the work you have to do after you get your tenants in place. The cost of managing everything yourself or hiring a manager, etc. We'll discuss those things in greater detail in a later chapter.

How you profit from your investment will really depend on what you are able to put into it. The profit potential you will make will depend just as much on your investment in yourself as it will in the property. But, it is true, the profit potential for investing in rental property can be quite high. Even if you are not looking to rake in millions of dollars, you will at least be able to rely on a steady stream of income monthly that will carry you through all the difficult economic times. As a matter of fact, you'll probably have a healthy flow of cash coming in even during those lean years for everyone else.

The Demand

The reality is simple. Everyone needs to have a home or at least a home base. So, if you're thinking of catering to the masses, there will always be a need for what you have to offer if you invest in real estate. Profits are a true example of supply and demand. No matter what conditions exist throughout the world, people will always need a place to stay. As a property owner, your money comes from meeting the demands of the public.

Still, not to get too excited about it, you cannot make a fortune on just any property you find. In order for you to realize the potential of real estate investing, you have to get into the market at or below market value. Thus, you can capitalize on the appreciation of the property, any improvements you have to make, and the rental income it will generate.

Be Realistic

Before we go any further, there is one very important fundament that you must know and understand. If you're up late at night, watching those infomercials that are promising you millions of dollars on a $20 investment and you're buying into it, then you're up for a disappointment. This book is not a get-rich-quick scheme that will teach you how to put in little investment money, even less effort, and come out on top. Those ideas, while they sound promising, are mostly fairy tales. Yes, there is the occasional guy who manages to luck into some good deals but how confident are you, that you are that person?

For the rest of the world, yes, you can make a good sum of money in real estate, but you won't do it while sitting on the beach in Cabo sipping margaritas; especially in the beginning. In the real world, you're going to need to invest just as much discipline and time into the project as you will money. Once you get the ball rolling, you'll have to continue pushing until your real estate machine starts working for itself. After that, it will become much easier and eventually, you'll see it evolve into something you will be able to retire on and live life the way you want. But don't plan on that happening automatically. If that's what you're looking for then you won't find that here in this book.

Chapter 2: Let's Talk About Money

When the economy is struggling, people tend to flee from investing in those non-tangible assets as a way to preserve their cash. Stock markets tend to be too volatile for some and other investment tools can seem quite questionable when the economy is rocky. As a result, many turn to one of the few tangible assets they can find. Real Estate. It is a hard asset that can be used to protect them from the constant ebb and flow of the various markets.

There is an inborn drive to protect oneself from a threat to one's livelihood. Because of the huge housing debacle that started back in 2008, real estate has never been easier to get into. With many properties being sold by banks and financial institutions at prices lower than ever, finding a good piece of property to invest in is the easy part. What's hard is determining how much capital it will take to get started.

To make this decision, there are several options that offer you a foot-in-the-door approach to the real estate market and how much money you need will depend on which option you choose.

Cost Get Started

If you don't have thousands of dollars to make a down payment in real estate, it doesn't mean you can't invest. One of the lowest cost options in real estate is to start with a Real Estate Investment Trust (REIT). REITs were started back in the 1960s offering an opportunity for the average investor to get a small piece of the commercial real estate world. These are companies that rent larger properties like shopping malls, hospitals, warehouses, etc. You can purchase a share in a REIT on the major exchanges like the NYSE or the NASDAQ. The cost of a single share can range in price from as little as $5 up to several hundreds. In exchange for your investment dollars, REITs will pay a regular dividend, which means that you can start to receive a steady return on your investment, almost immediately.

To get started investing in REITs, you don't need a lot of capital. Some even offer a dividend reinvestment plan (DRIPs) that will automatically take your returns and reinvest them to grow your capital. You can start with buying as little as one share and grow from there. So, if you only have a few dollars to start, you can grow your investment there. If you have a little more, then you could start with a mutual fund company with a low starting investment of around $500.

If you're more determined to get into owning physical property and you don't have a lot of capital to put up, you can consider getting started with a Real Estate Investment Group (REIG). These are organizations that purchase groups of properties and then resells them to investors for rental properties. The REIG will assist you in finding tenants, handling the maintenance of the properties, and managing other responsibilities and in return, they take a percentage of the rent you collect as payment.

With a REIG, you can purchase one or more apartment or condominium complexes. All of the details will be managed for you and at the end of the month, you can collect the rent. As an investor, you are the owner of the property but at a much lower cost than if you bought the unit outright. To get started investing in a REIG, you will need at least $5,000. Of course, that amount is not enough to purchase an entire unit, but you could become a part of a pool of multiple investors that share ownership, which could return you a nice little monthly cash flow, which you could build up until you have enough cash to make a full purchase.

A step up from that is actual property ownership and becoming a tried and true landlord. For this type of investment, you will need to have at least enough cash on hand for a decent down payment or enough credit to get financing. The general requirement is 20% down plus closing costs, which usually will run around $5000. Then you will need enough cash flow to get the property up to rentable condition.

In the end, the amount of money you need to get started with will depend largely on how much capital you have. If you're a big dreamer with a small wallet, then you can start generating income through a REIT, but if you have a significant amount of savings or you have access to ready cash then you can start right into buying property outright.

Of course, these are not the only real estate opportunities for you to take advantage of. They are just examples of the lower end investment opportunities all the way up to the higher end. So, in the end, how much money you need will depend on where you are starting but that does not in any way limit where you will end up.

Hidden Costs

In order to make money in real estate, it is very important that you understand the numbers. While real estate investing can be very profitable, there are quite a few moving parts that you have to be aware of. If you are not careful, each of those parts can leach out the profits you expect to have. It is very easy to make money in real estate, but it is also very easy to lose it. You need to be educated in order to make sure that you know how to protect your assets before you get started. It does not mean that you have to go back to school, but you need to know enough to do the research and apply the principles you learn to ensure that your investment will produce positive results

Know the Numbers

When you are dealing with real estate, a lot of money is changing hands. You need to know your expected cash flow at all times. Not just in terms of how much you expect to receive but also in how much is going out. It involves a lot more than the purchase price, as there are hidden costs in almost everything you do. One of the main reasons why people lose money in real estate is because they are not aware of this monetary traffic. They know how much they can expect to receive in terms of income, but they fail to anticipate how much it's going to cost to keep the property in good working condition.

This is especially true if you're planning on flipping houses. The novice thinks about the costs of materials, labor, and permits but fails to think about the investment in time. They often underestimate how long it will take to get the work done; in the meantime, for every day over the expected time frame, they are losing money while spending for additional costs for that same time period. In such cases, you need to know:

- What the value of the property will be after the rehab.
- How much rent to charge to recoup that expense

- And how much cushion you should have access to if the project should run overtime

There is no way you can reasonably determine whether an investment is going to be worth your time and money if you don't do your homework.

If you feel you are handy, you also need to factor in the additional costs of doing the work yourself. Don't fool yourself into thinking that you can do all the work yourself and save a bundle of money. Unless you have the unique skills and qualifications to do this type of work, you may actually end up losing money.

It is easy to look at a contractor's estimate and assume that you could save a bundle by doing it on your own. However, chances are you're already holding down a job so you can pay for the property and meet the mortgage payments. Thus, you don't have a lot of time to invest in the work even if you do have the skills. As a result, the project will take a lot longer to complete than you may have anticipated.

Other costs, that new investors fail to recognize:

- The time it takes to find good tenants
- The time it takes to collect rents, do the paperwork, and the banking
- Property visits to make sure tenants are maintaining it
- Managing repairs, landscaping, and other incidentals.

There are also the hidden costs associated with unrealized gains. You may have invested in the property in the hopes that the value would increase within a certain time frame or after some work is done. If this does not happen within your timetable, are you prepared to continue with the property until it appreciates in value?

The costs associated with a market slump. Real estate investing is a very profitable one but like any other investment opportunity. One cannot expect the cost to steadily rise year over year without some fallback. Only invest in those properties that will consistently earn money regardless of the economic cycle.

There are lots of hidden costs that may come up in real estate investing, each one can catch you by surprise and knock you out of the game before you realize it. To make a true success of real estate investing there are no shortcuts. You have to do your homework, review it, and then do it again. Hidden costs are everywhere and you need to keep your eyes on the numbers every step of the way. The rewards are there only if you're ready to work for them.

Getting the Best Financing

OK, now let's say you've found the property you want to invest in. You've done your homework, checked everything out for those hidden costs, and even formulated a reasonable working plan that will get you the keys to the property. All that's left to do now, is secure the financing.

There is a lot to know about real estate financing. Unless you're rolling in cash from the get-go, your financing will be the most expensive part of your investment, but not all of the opportunities will be right for you. The plan that will work best will depend on where you are in the financial scheme of things. Let's look at some options and what each requires for you to qualify.

Pay in Cash

If you are looking to buying a distressed property, you might find one low enough in cost that you can pay the full amount in cash. Even if you have a boatload of money to put into the property, you still need to know your numbers. Paying cash is not always the smartest way to buy a home. The return on investment may not be worth the money you put in.

For example, you have $100,000 in cash and you find a nice little home you can buy for it. You pay the money plus the extra costs to get it ready for rental and then you find a tenant to pay you $1,200/month to live there. At that rate, it will take you nearly 7 years to get your initial investment back and that's if you can keep a tenant there for the full 7 years. The figures don't include the amount of money you will spend on repairs and maintenance.

However, if you were to get bank financing, and use that same $100,000 as a down payment on four different homes, you would have a total mortgage payment of $400,000. However, if each of those homes was rented out for $1,200/month you would have a regular income of $6000/month or $72,000/year. Of course, you would probably only net around $400/month in cash after making your mortgage payments, which would leave your net earnings around $19,200/year. A huge difference between paying cash and financing. If you don't mind taking on a mortgage it could increase your profit potential exponentially, and you're building up equity in the property at the same time.

Traditional Mortgage

The most common way to finance property is through a traditional mortgage. As you saw in the above example, it can significantly increase your profit potential. By applying a cash down payment, with a traditional mortgage you can begin earning capital on your investment relatively quickly. It is important, however, to know that with these types of loans, you will be expected to have a minimum of 20% of the purchase price for a down payment, and with some types of investment properties as much as 25-30% of the purchase price.

Portfolio Lenders

Most traditional mortgages come from banks and financial institutions. However, they are not your only option in raising capital for your property. You could also get financing from portfolio lenders. At first glance, they may appear to be the same as a traditional mortgage but there is a difference.

With a traditional mortgage, the financial institution is not lending you their own money but is instead using funding from other sources; a government-backed company like Fannie Mae or Freddie Mac, for example. It is why their lending standards are usually pretty strict and loans are often difficult to qualify for.

However, there are some financial institutions that have their own funds to lend. In such cases, they can afford to be laxer on the lending requirements so it may be much easier to qualify. In other words, they can frame their terms based on their own requirements rather than on an outside institution. For those who may have difficulty getting credit for a traditional bank loan, a portfolio lender may be able to help them.

FHA Loans

FHA stands for the Federal Housing Administration and is a government-backed program that insures mortgages for the banks. They actually pool money from different sources so that the risk is spread out. FHA loans are created for property where the borrower will be living on the property and are not offered as a financing option for investment property exclusively. However, they do have a clause that allows the purchaser to have as many as four different units on the property. So, if you choose to live in one unit, then you are free to rent out the other three. FHA loans are easier to get because they require a lower down payment (around 3.5%) but you will also be required to make an additional "Private Mortgage Insurance" payment to protect the lender in case you default.

203K Loans

Another aspect of the FHA loan is the 203K. A 203K is a loan that permits the homeowner to purchase a house that needs work done. With this type of loan, you are able to finance the property and the repairs all at the same time. With the 203K, you can still make a lower down payment, but with an additional requirement; for the life of the loan you remain an owner occupant on the property.

Home Equity Loans/Lines of Credit

If you are already a property owner, many institutions will allow you to borrow money based on the equity you have built up in your property. To qualify for your home equity loan, you have to already own property and have built up equity in it. The amount of the loan will depend on how much value you hold in the property and the percentage of that equity the bank is willing to lend on. Most institutions will offer up to 90% of the total value of the home.

Alternative Financing Options

In addition to the standard financing options, you can also take advantage of a few alternative financing options available. If for some reason, you are not able to get traditional financing, there are plenty of other ways to get the cash you need to get started.

Owner Financing

You may be able to strike a deal with the owner of the property. These are usually pretty easy to do. You simply make your payments to the owner rather than the financial institution. The trick here is to find an owner who is willing to work with you in this way. In most cases, this will only happen if the owner owns the property outright. In other words, they do not have an existing mortgage that needs to be paid off on the property. If the owner has a mortgage or a lien on the property, he or she may demand that you give him at least a down payment that will pay those loans off completely, otherwise you may be getting a property that is about to go into foreclosure.

This usually happens with loans that carry a "Due on Sale" clause, demanding that if they sell the property at any time, they must pay the debt in full with the proceeds from the sale. If they are unable to pay the balance of the mortgage, then foreclosure proceedings will begin.

There are some exceptions to this rule, so anytime you are negotiating an owner financing deal, you must be very careful to read the fine print before any money exchanges hands or any agreements are signed.

Under the right circumstances, owner financing can be a great alternative way to get ownership of real property and bypass the bank at the same time. It could also be a good way to quickly sell off property in the future.

Hard Money Lending

Hard Money financing or private financing is when you acquire the funds from a private business or individual. This financing option is where you can get quite creative in your financing options. Hard money lending will suffice in the short-term, but you may have to pay a higher than average interest rate. If you are struggling with credit, this is a great option as most lenders do not check credit nor do they look at your income as a basis for the loan. Instead, they will look at the overall value of the property and what the value of the rehab work will take if you plan to flip it.

These are great for short-term loans but exercise this option with caution. Because they are usually for a very short period of time, it is strongly advised that you have a good backup plan in case there is a delay in completing your project and you are unable to fulfill the payment as originally agreed.

Private Money

Another option that is similar to hard money is through a private lender. Here you are working with an individual who is looking for another way to get a higher return on their investment. With this type of lender, there are fewer additional costs or the stringent requirements that institutions often ask.

They will lend you cash money in exchange for a set interest rate. The agreement is secured with a promissory note giving them the right to foreclose if you don't pay. These loans can be both long and short-term with terms as short as six months all the way up to thirty years.

Partnerships

If you have a good working relationship with someone else, you can form a partnership together. Taking on an equity partner can be a very profitable idea. You are free to structure the agreement any way you can between the two of you, there are no set guidelines and no stringent requirements to be met. Just make sure that you create a legal operating agreement and both parties sign. The agreement should detail each party's role, how the agreement is put together, those responsible for making decisions, and the division of profits.

In most cases, the partner, whether taking an active or a passive role, does not receive any interest payments like an outright lender but is entitled to a share of the income the property generates.

Commercial Loans

When purchasing rental property, most people do not realize that a commercial loan may be their best option. While the majority of residential loans require you to live in the property while paying the mortgage, if you're planning on purchasing a property that has more than four units, you may qualify for a commercial loan.

Commercial loans are generally for shorter terms than a residential one and offer higher interest rates, but it may be an easier loan to get. Since the income of the borrower is not usually the deciding factor, the value of the property gets primary consideration. While they may look at your income, credit history, and personal finances, it is usually only as a guide to tell them how you manage money and not whether or not you have the resources to pay the loan back.

Commercial loans are an excellent option for those who are interested in flipping houses. They offer a business line of credit to help finance these extensive remodeling needs, which can give you a pool of resources to tap into in order to get the job done faster than usual.

It is quite obvious that the days of getting loans from financial institutions is not the only resource you have. Often, if you are smart you will look at all your options before making a final decision on which type of financing you want. There are pros and cons to each option, so take your time and look at all the details before you make a final decision.

One thing you want to avoid is rushing into things. Just because you are able to secure financing for a new project doesn't mean that it is the right decision for you. As we've already discussed, hidden fees are everywhere. Examine every offer closely and read between the lines. Whatever deal you make to finance your new real estate project. Make sure you are entering it completely with your eyes wide open.

Contract Flipping

Flipping contracts is a savvy real estate investment strategy where you first locate a property where you are confident you can secure an agreement from the seller and you are sure you can find a buyer for the property at a much higher price. The profit you earn is not based on interest rates, rental income, or equity value but in the difference between the price you agreed upon with the seller and the price you get from the buyer.

Flipping contracts is a lot like playing the role of a realtor, except that you purchase the contract with the sole purpose of flipping them. In order for this strategy to work, there are several things you must have in order first.

1. Make sure there is an agreement with the homeowner allowing you to exit the contract without losing any money that you have put up as a deposit.
2. You must also be confident that you can find a buyer to take over the contract and close the sale. If you cannot, then you may find that you are responsible for closing the sale yourself.
3. Once the buyer is secured, the contract is closed, and you can pocket the difference.

While flipping a contract is not the same as an outright purchase of property or getting financing, if you are successful, you can return a pretty hefty profit on any property in a very short period of time.

Chapter 3: Getting Started

You've made the decision to take your chances with real estate but now you have no idea how to begin. One of the first questions you need to answer is what type of investment property is right for you. You have a lot of options to choose from when it comes to types of rental property. Apartments, condos, single-family properties, complexes, commercial real estate, and a lot more. While many people may tell you they prefer one over the other, the one that you should choose should be based on your personal circumstances.

Decide on What You Want

Before you make your decision, it's time for some personal reflection. Ask yourself:

- o What are your goals?
- o What is the market like

- Where can you find the best deals?

Only you know your community and what kind of opportunities await you. We'll go through some basic things to look for as you consider each of the rental options that may be available.

Single or Multifamily Units

Most people would prefer the multifamily units because they feel that these will generate a lot more income than a single-family unit. With a multifamily unit you have the potential for greater income, however, you also have a lot more work involved. If you plan on managing the property yourself and not hiring a management company to do it for you, then maybe single-family units would be a better option.

If you have the time to dedicate to the property, and the resources to keep a maintenance crew on hand, then a multifamily unit may work. You have to take the time to evaluate your personal circumstances to decide which option will suit your life and goals best. While you may have big dreams with lots of dollar signs in your eyes, it is very important for you to be honest with your personal appraisal of yourself. The best investment option for you will depend on what you are capable of handling, how much commitment you have, and what you realistically can expect to gain.

It is not enough to find a single-family unit at market value. If you really hope to turn a profit in this industry, start from the beginning looking for those properties that are selling below market value. It is the main reason you'll get excellent returns on your rentals. Some real estate experts will only look at properties that are selling at 70-80% below market value. These are usually fixer-uppers and have been that way for an extended period of time.

When you can find property below market value, you make money in two ways. First, your property value goes up as soon as you close because you bought below market, but you will also add value from the improvements you make. Add to that, the rental income if you decide to lease the units and you have a pretty easy steady income in your future.

Making a Plan

It can be tempting to get an idea and then jump right into a real estate purchase. With your mind focused on the bottom line, it is easy to forget the practical steps. You want to get in and get started as fast as you can. While you may luck out and find a good deal, it is also a pretty easy way to put yourself on the fast track to disaster. The best way to avoid this kind of failure is to build your own real estate business plan.

Unlike the regular property owner, you won't just buy one piece of property and you're done. If you're really interested in developing a real estate empire, you will be jumping from one great opportunity to the next. You'll probably be pretty successful for the first one or two properties but after that, things can get quite complicated.

As you create your plan there are a few things you need to include.

- o Your purpose for investing
    - o A dream vacation
    - o Improve your quality of life
    - o Build a retirement fund
    - o Your child's university education

Without a sense of direction, it can be very difficult to stay focused. You will end up looking at investments that won't help you achieve your plans.

After you've determined your purpose, your next step should be to decide on what type of investments you're going to be focused on. There are many options, some of them we will be discussing in detail in the next chapter, but here are a few that you may not have considered.

- o Student rentals
- o Multi-family rentals
- o Rent to own properties

- Vacation rentals
- Flipping houses

The key reason for developing a plan is to treat your real estate investments as you would a real business. If you're planning on using this for income, it will actually be a true business and you should start with this approach in mind from the very beginning.

Every business plan regardless of the kind of business it represents must have clear intentions on what the investor hopes to do, what they hope to get out of it, and why they want to do it. Writing out your plan is not just to help you remember these things, but it is also a way to keep your eyes trained on your end goal.

But this does not mean that you have to write out a complex and detailed plan complete with financial statements, tax records, or other complicated documents in order to get started. It could be as simple as writing out a to-do list so that you don't miss out on any details. Starting out, you first list your major milestones and then break each milestone down into smaller and smaller manageable steps.

To help you get started here is a basic outline you can follow:

1. Mission Statement
    a. What is your business?
    b. What kind of benefits will you provide?
    c. What is the purpose of your business
        i. I want to _____ for _____
2. Vision
    a. Where do you see yourself in the future?
        i. What is your dream?
        ii. Mental Picture
            1. My business will _____ by _____ in 5 years
            2. Create a vision board
3. Goals
    a. What do you hope to achieve with your real estate investing

       i. This may seem like the same thing as Step 2 but here you want to go into more detail. Be very specific

      ii. Examples:
1. To get a nicer home
2. A dream vacation to Fiji
3. Retirement fund
4. Go back to school
5. Travel the world

4. Time Frame
    a. Set a specific timeline for each goal
    b. Prioritize
5. Type of Property
    a. Student Rentals
    b. Multi-family
    c. Rent to Own
    d. Starter Homes
    e. Buy and Hold
    f. Tiny Homes
    g. Container Homes

    h. Collapsible Homes

    i. Flips

        i. Choose one to focus on

        ii. Master the strategy before starting another

6. Rules

    a. Rules to look for deals

        i. Distance from home – Only consider properties within 20 minutes from home

        ii. No HOA fees

        iii. Cash flow minimum

        iv. No underground tans

        v. # of bedrooms

        vi. 1+ bathrooms

7. Market

    a. Location – Neighborhood

    b. Know the area

    c. Travel time

    d. Travel expenses

8. Team
    a. Who is on your team
    b. Business Partners
    c. Support system
        i. Banker
        ii. Lawyer
        iii. Insurance broker
        iv. Home inspector
        v. Realtor
        vi. Property manager
9. Financials
    a. Investment capital
    b. Where is the money coming from
        i. Live in while fixing
        ii. Home Equity
        iii. Cash
        iv. Securities
        v. Business Partners
10. Exit Strategy
    a. How will you collect money

    b. Pay off mortgage

    c. Rent

    d. Flip

    e. Rehab

    f. Rent to own

        i. Always have more than one strategy

When you break up your business plan into sections like the example above, it won't feel so overwhelming and you can take it in small bite-sized pieces that are easily manageable. As you gain more experience in real estate, you will find that your plans will become more detailed but easier at the same time.

Types of Rental Property

There are many different ways you can turn a real estate investment into a profitable empire. You might think only of rental property, which is definitely a profitable venture, but it is not the only option. It is important for you to know each of the many different opportunities, so you can decide which one will work best for you. The more familiar you are with different investment options the easier it will be to determine if a property is going to fit into your plan or not.

Flipping

With all the TV shows now, many people are very excited about flipping houses. Finding a distressed property at a discount and then improving it and reselling seems like a real easy way to make some fast money. When you fix and flip, you find a home that is structurally sound but needs some cosmetic work in order to bring up its resale value. It could be something as simple as a nice coat of paint all the way up to refinishing the floors, upgrading the kitchen or lighting fixtures.

Flipping properties is a great way for beginners to enter the real estate game. It comes with a very low risk because you can usually find homes that have been abandoned and get them at ridiculously low prices. After putting in a little extra cash, you can turn quite a sizable profit in just a matter of a few months.

Older homes and foreclosures are usually the most popular choices, but you don't have to limit yourself to these areas. These work great especially if you have any kind of skills in carpentry, electrical, plumbing, etc. It will save you from having to pay a contractor to do the work if you're willing to put in a little elbow grease.

Rehabbing

Similar to flipping houses, rehab involves fixing up a property for either sale or rental. Rehab projects are a lot more extensive and can require a great deal of work to bring the building up to code. It could include a complete rewiring, replumbing, changing the entire layout of the home, or even replacing the foundation.

Generally, rehabs fall into three different categories. Each category carries a different level of risk.

Rehabbing for personal use	Lowest risk
Rehabbing for rental	Medium risk
Rehabbing for resale	Highest risk

For the beginner, it is best to start with your lowest risk option, which is rehabbing for personal use. As long as you live in the house while making the necessary repairs and upgrades, you do not have the added expense of maintaining a second property. You also don't have the same pressure to have it finished by a certain date, which could ease up a lot on the stress level. When you're flipping on the other hand, for every day the property is not on the market, you're losing a little money. Delays in such cases could end up being catastrophic.

It also allows you the time to learn as you go. No matter how much research and planning go into preparing for a rehab, you're always going to hit roadblocks. It's part of life in the real estate business. You're going to make mistakes but it's a lot easier to deal with those mistakes if you're not under the gun to complete a project within a set time period.

If you choose to rehab, don't start off with a super big project, look for one that will ensure that you make some money. You don't want a life-changing project where you earn a million dollars the first time out of the gate. Start small and build up as you go. With both flipping and rehab, your profit is realized by the increase in the value of the home after you have completed the work.

Rental Property

Rental property is using the property to receive a regular payment from those who choose to rent or lease. It is a great way to make a steady income. Unlike flipping where you fix and sell, you will receive smaller payments over an extended period of time.

There are several ways in which you can make money through rentals. If you buy and hold the property you can rent it out for the long term. This method will give you a consistently steady flow of income that could last you for years.

Another way you can make money on rental properties is to offer the home on a rent-to-own plan. This system is where the renter gives you a down payment and then pays you rent with the specific agreement that a percentage of the rent will be applied to the sale price of the home. At an agreed upon time, the renter can either return the property to you or pay it off based on the terms of the contract.

You are not limited to renting out apartments and homes. You can also rent out condos, townhouses, commercial property, and even land. With either option, you will receive a monthly income that can be applied to the mortgage, interest, and any maintenance needed to keep the property in livable condition.

Mobile Homes

This is a real estate investment option that few people think about. If you have structure-less property, you can rent out a permanent spot for a mobile home to be placed. These are usually single-family units. Many are surprised to learn that mobile homes are one of the fastest growing types of housing in the nation. Because the traditional home is often far out-priced for the average person, a mobile home looks and feels like a real home but at a far lower cost.

It is a common practice to find a mobile home and then resell it for twice what you may have paid for it. It is a low-risk investment and a great way to offer a rent to own feature. You can make even more money on the interest you will collect on the monthly payment.

Commercial

Few people actually think about investing in commercial property and yet they are one of the most rewarding investment opportunities out there. Commercial properties can include anything from warehouses, office spaces, or any other property that is used exclusively for business.

There are several segments of this type of real estate you can work in. It covers a whole gambit of opportunities including industrial, agricultural, hospitality, medical facilities, marinas, laboratories, and so on. You can even offer up a patch of farmland. You will need to become familiar with these types of businesses so that you can accurately evaluate the actual value of the property and how it can be used as an asset to that particular type of business.

For the new investor, it is probably best to tread in waters you are most familiar with. Apartment complexes, multi-tenant retail, and office spaces, and even self-storage facilities. The knowledge needed to operate these types of facilities is not as extensive and you have fewer pitfalls you can run into.

One of the biggest draws with dealing in commercial property is that you will be able to earn a lot more money for the same size floor space in a residential property. You will be able to build strong professional connections in the business world that will take you a lot further in your real estate plan than you would with just dealing with residential property.

Foreclosures

Investing in foreclosures is a great way to get your foot in the real estate door. It will allow you to earn more money faster than a traditional real estate purchase. You will pay a lower price for the same property and will be free and clear that much faster.

There are three ways to invest in foreclosures. First, you could buy directly from the homeowner who is facing foreclosure. Your intervention would allow him to prevent that step and save his credit and give you a good deal at the same time. You can also buy from a lender who has recently foreclosed on the property, or finally, you can buy a home at an auction.

The only way to clear a profit on a foreclosure is to pay off the remaining debt and then resell at a higher price. You may be able to work out a short sale so that you can get the property for less than what is owed, which would put you further ahead profit wise.

Of course, there may be many other ways to make money in real estate and these are just a few you should pay attention to. In time, you'll uncover some of the least obvious ways to invest and may even be brave enough to try some of the more risky options to get a profit.

However, for the purposes of this book, we will focus on just these ones for beginning investors.

Setting Up Bank Accounts

In order for your money to flow freely in real estate, you need to have a strong relationship with your banking partners. A strong, lasting relationship is more important in this industry than in any other. You will soon discover that you will rely on your bank for many aspects of your business. Aside from paying contractors, realtors and other services, you will depend on you will need several different banking accounts to keep your business afloat. Thus, you need to be very careful in selecting a bank that will manage your business accounts. It would be smart to learn how to negotiate for the best interest rates you can find.

Interest Rates

Being able to negotiate a low-interest rate, good credit terms will be crucial to the success of your business. Interest rate spreads and other alternative financing plans can vary wildly from one institution to another, especially when dealing with business. It is important to minimize the risk of exposure to fluctuations in these costs. You might want to consider getting interest rate protection to lower your risk of volatile changes that could impact your long-term rates on accounts when they are at their lowest.

Tax Strategies

A good relationship with your bank can also help you save up on your taxes. They can offer you practical advice on how best to execute real estate transactions that can give you major tax advantages. For example, they may suggest a tax-deferred property exchange where you can swap one piece of property for another of similar value, all while deferring the need to pay federal income taxes until you are ready. In such a case, the income tax for the exchange of property would not be due until the property you received in the exchange is sold and you have a lot more money in your account to pay them.

Lines of Credit

Another way you can work with your bank is through a line of credit. While you may get your funding from any number of sources, you will still have to pay for your expenses through your bank account. You can establish a regular line of credit through them to cover any expenses related to property renovations, the closing costs, and other expenses that will be a part of your business. A small company with a strong credit history and a long-standing relationship with their bank can go a lot further than one that is bouncing from one account to another.

Mortgage Loans

Unless you have loads of cash in hand, you're probably going to need to get a mortgage to pay for your properties. If you're doing traditional financing, you'll need to have a good relationship with your bank. Before you choose a bank, try to find out as much as you can about how the bank handles mortgages. Because real estate mortgages are likely the highest form of income for the bank, you want to know what kind of relationship they can offer. If you can forge a solid bond, it can be a win-win for both parties. Don't accept their first offer but be willing to negotiate for a better interest rate, easier payment plans, and lower fees. Don't accept if the terms are not right for you.

Chapter 4: Where to Find Property

Now, that you've got all your ducks in a row, it's time to go shopping. You know about the different benefits of real estate and you're ready to take the plunge. You have established a good relationship with your bank and you've got your financing at least in the preliminary stages. All you need to do now is find your first piece of property. But where should you look?

Finding Property

If you've been a renter up until now, you already know that there is more than one way to find a rental. But things can be a little different when you're looking for a place to buy. You obviously won't be looking in the same places for properties to buy, but there can be some overlapping. However, with real estate, there are some places that a renter would never go to find a place to live. Let's take a look at these places first.

Real Estate Auctions

There are many places where real estate is auctioned off. Most of the properties sold at auction are foreclosures. You can find some of the lowest prices at these sites. There are live auctions and online auctions so depending on the type of property you're interested in, you'll have to participate with either one of them.

One of the first places to look is online or in your local newspaper. Before you engage in an auction, you first need to learn the rules of the auction site. If you're looking in a newspaper, there should be some type of legal notice of any upcoming auctions. Make a note of the auction companies so you can visit their website directly to find out about what their requirements are to enter.

Government Websites

Foreclosed properties can also be found on several government websites. They maintain a listing of upcoming auctions for properties that have outstanding taxes due. These are properties that weren't foreclosed on because of not paying their mortgage but from not paying their taxes. You can find some pretty affordable properties here for a song.

Fannie Mae will first try to sell their own foreclosed properties before they put them up for auction. However, if for some reason they are unable to sell it the traditional way, they will put it up for auction through HomePath.com.

You can also check the U.S. Department of Agriculture and the Federal Deposit Insurance Corporation for properties they may be planning to auction.

The U.S. Treasury: https://www.treasury.gov/auctions/treasury/rp/.

Fannie Mae foreclosures through Home Path:

https://www.homepath.com/investors.html

Your Bank

Some banks have an inventory of properties on their website. These lists can be found by doing a Google search with the name of the bank and the term "REO" which means Real Estate Owned or bank-owned.

Zillow.com

This has a list of properties for sale. Their filtering option allows you to narrow down your search to only include foreclosed or rehabbed properties

Real Estate Broker

You can never go wrong by asking a real estate broker for possible auctions in your area.

Find Absentee Owners

Another, more creative way to find property is to approach an absentee owner of the property and make a private deal. With a competitive market like real estate, sometimes listed properties are receiving multiple offers that you may have little or no chance of getting into. Sometimes your best shot is to get to a property before it is listed.

An absentee owner is an individual who owns a property but lives elsewhere. They may be a landlord or they may have inherited the property from someone. This approach may take a bit of work, but it can certainly pay off in the end. You can find these properties by:

- Driving around a neighborhood looking for vacant homes
- Online public records can help you find the owner
- Buy a public record listing from a source like ListSource.com

- Calling owners of places for rent

When it comes down to it, finding the right property to buy is a numbers game. The more properties you look at, the better your chances of finding something that will pay off in the end.

Choosing the Right Property

Once you have your listings, you should collect several properties to look at, so you can evaluate and compare. The priority now is determining which property will be a good investment. Reaching a conclusion will not always be easy due to the numerous factors for you to consider.

You will need to know exactly what you plan to do with the property. If you're purchasing rental properties, there are different factors to consider as opposed to purchasing property to flip or rehab.

For Rental Property

Your strategy here should be about finding something that you can be comfortable with. When looking at property, avoid thinking only about the risk. While that is important, there are many other things to consider when deciding on a rental property. Many new investors start off by expecting to find a perfect unit straight out of the gate, but this is rarely the case. You can expect, even in a well-structured building that you're going to have to do some work to get it up to speed.

In addition to getting the property below market value, with these types of properties you also have to factor in the cost of maintenance, managing the property, and cost of repairs, vacancies and a host of other things. To help you to decide if the property is right for you, here are a few basic guidelines.

- **Single-Family Residence:** These are considered the best option for a new investor. If you already own a home then you already have a good idea of the costs to keep it maintained for a renter. This information makes the initial evaluation of the property relatively easy. You also need to factor in the cost of water and sewer hook-up if it hasn't already been included. The only decision you have to make beyond the estimate of costs is whether you want long-term renters or vacation renters. There are several advantages to this type of rental property. First of all, you only have to deal with one responsible party for the rent, so it is easy to keep records. You can include the cost of utilities in the rent or have your tenant accept responsibility for these additional expenses. And it is only one structure, so you do not have a lot of buildings that need to be maintained. If you don't have a lot of time to manage a property, then this type of investment may be your best option.

However, even in single-family dwellings, you are likely to be responsible for maintaining the exterior, which includes the lawn and landscaping. If you were to purchase a condo or a townhome, then you would be paying HOA fees that will also have to be factored into the overall costs. Make sure you budget for vacancy periods. With only one unit as your income, vacancies can hit your pocketbook pretty hard.

- **Duplex/Triplex:** These multifamily units can make a huge difference financially when compared to a single-family dwelling. You can live in one unit and rent out the others saving you on expenses. Make sure that you can collect enough rent to cover both the unit you are living in and the one you're renting out. If you choose a triplex, you also have a little cushion in case of a vacancy.

  Depending on the location, these can work great in university towns or areas where many singles tend to live. The expenses are easily managed, and you still only have one building to maintain.

Still, you will have additional expenses to contend with. You will be responsible for several meters for utility services or have to create a way to manage these expenses so that they are fair for all concerned.

- **Apartments:** Purchasing an apartment building may not be as easy an investment to get into as the other options. These can easily run up into the millions of dollars and getting enough credit to cover the cost can be quite difficult. However, if you have an apartment building in your sites it may be best to approach the project with a partner or a group to help you foot the bill. If you can, there are plenty of benefits that make good reasons to pursue apartment rentals.

As a first time investor, consider starting out with a smaller apartment building with four to ten units. These are much easier to get into for an individual investor, but you will have a lot more risks associated with it. If you go in with a partner you will have a lower risk and you have more protection from vacancies. If one unit is empty, there is still enough wiggle room to make a clean profit.

On the other hand, if you have multiple units empty you can incur severe losses, especially if the condition continues for an extended period of time. Factor in additional maintenance expenses and consider having tenants responsible for their own utilities to make it easier.

- **Condos:** Condos, like apartments, can be rented out. These actually make for great vacation rentals but expect to pay additional HOA fees in addition to other expenses. If this is your plan, make sure vacation rentals are allowed in the building. Some

HOAs do not permit them so you want to check this out before you buy.

Keep in mind, that the HOA has the final say as to what kind of upgrades and changes you can make on the property. You may be restricted as to installing internet, satellites, or even what colors you are allowed to paint. There is also the issue of the neighbors, which could also restrict you on what liberties you can take with your unit as to rental property.

- **Commercial Property:** If you are interested in purchasing a commercial property keep in mind that your tenants will be businesses. On the surface, these can appear to be very lucrative opportunities, but it is best that you proceed cautiously. In recent years, we have seen many brick and mortar businesses fail because of competition from online stores, which offer a lot more convenience. When evaluating these types of properties, you need to think in an even wider scope. Learn the fundamentals of the business as well as their ability to turn a profit. Think about their competition, not just locally but online as well, their reputation in the community, and their product or service. All of these will have a bearing on your bottom line when they rent from you. The good news is that business tenants tend to pay more in rent than a residential tenant. If you acquire an entire building, you can have the benefit of multiple tenants paying rent, thus increasing the amount of revenue you can generate.

You will have additional expenses to factor in. By law, you will have to maintain a commercial property-liability insurance plan, which can be quite costly. There will be a high initial outlay of cash to buy the property, which may mean that you will have to take on a partner or a group of partners to fund the project. Maintenance expenses will be higher and there is still the expenses of vacancy periods, which are often more difficult to fill in commercial property.

When trying to decide which type of investment property is right for you, your number one concern is expenses. Unlike when you are dealing with an individual purchase for personal use, there are many factors that need to be weighed in order to find the right property. At the very least, factor in all expenses, add in another 10-20% for those unexpected ones and then weigh those against the potential income the property will generate.

This is much harder if you're looking at flipping houses or rehabs. There are, of course, those obvious costs, but often in such buildings, additional surprises come up that could easily curtail your project. By taking all of those into consideration, evaluating how much time and money you have to invest, you can narrow down your options and find the right property to invest in.

About Vacation Rentals

It is estimated that the vacation rental industry is expected to generate $36.6 billion for the coming year. This figure is partly due to the fact that travelers have discovered that they can pay the same amount of money as an expensive hotel and get a more home-like experience with additional space and amenities to boot.

Vacation rentals can be a highly lucrative investment option but there are a few things you need to keep in mind before you decide to jump in and try your hand at this business.

- Vacation homes are just like any other hospitality business. You will take on a long-term responsibility, so you need to have your objectives clearly in mind.

- The location should be of primary importance. Finding a great deal in an area where tourists do not frequent won't get you very many guests to occupy your home. Look for properties in well-established areas where you can reasonably expect tourists will want to visit.
- Quality is paramount. Your guests will be paying prices comparable to a high-quality hotel, so they will expect accommodations that will be better than a standard home to live in. It doesn't need to be in a resort, but you will have to offer them something that will be a cut above the average living conditions they would normally receive at home.
- Mixed developments do not work well for vacation rentals. Vacationers are more comfortable with other vacationers, and full-time residents will feel more at ease if their neighbors are not changing every week.
- If you can hire a management company it can make a huge difference in vetting the guests before they

come to rent your place. Because the turn-over of occupancy changes frequently, they can handle all the little details that will ensure that your guests get the best experience possible. They can verify that payments are made and that the guests have something special that they will remember and talk about when they return home.

If you want to be a part of a growing industry, vacation rentals can generate far more cash flow per year than the average home rental. However, you will have to raise your standards considerably in order to attract the kind of clientele that will be willing to pay the premium prices that these kinds of rentals demand.

The Short Sale

When looking for that perfect deal on a piece of property, there are many roads you can take. Ideally, you are looking to find the property at the best price possible and one way to get a significant break in the expenses is through a short sale.

A short sale is when the homeowner agrees to sell his property for less than what is owed on the mortgage. You might wonder why a property owner would consider making such a deal. If he sells short, he could still be on the hook for the remaining balance on the mortgage.

While short sales are not as common as they once were, they are a great way to help homeowners who are underwater or behind in their mortgage payments. In other words, they find that they owe more on their homes than it is actually worth.

You can find short sale listings in the same place as you would find other property listings. Their posting will specifically say 'short sale or subject lender' so that potential buyers will know exactly what the homeowner is willing to accept.

When the buyer makes an offer, the homeowner cannot just accept the offer on his/her own. He has to take the offer to his bank and make an official request for a short sale status on the property. The bank then has the option to accept or reject the offer.

To get a short sale approved, the homeowner must file a number of documents including a hardship letter explaining why they are unable to repay the full amount of their mortgage. They will also have to give proof of their current financial status including pay stubs and tax returns. After the bank has reviewed the documentation, an appraiser has verified the full value of the property and the offer, they will make their decision.

When making a short sale offer, expect to have even closer scrutiny than normal. The bank will want to thoroughly vet you, calculate any risks they may be accepting and any potential opportunities.

Short sales are not the ideal solution for the homeowner, especially if they are suffering from financial difficulties, but it may be the best option. It also helps them to avoid foreclosure, which can be very damaging to their credit score. Thus, they can recover faster and will be in a better position to buy again in the future.

For the buyer, it can provide you with a property at a significant discount but at the same time, you will incur extra expenses that the homeowner usually has to pay. Expect to pay all the fees and charges that are connected to any home purchase. The cost includes agent commissions, which are normally paid by the bank, closing costs, inspections and so on.

Chapter 5: Buying the Property

If you've never purchased a piece of property before, some of the terms you've heard are probably pretty confusing. You might be wondering what it means to "close" the deal and why does it cost so much. In actuality, the closing is the process where the property changes hands. While you may have made an offer, written the check, gotten approval, and everything else, the property is not yours until it closes.

There are several steps that have to be taken into consideration when buying any type of property. While the details of the deal may vary, the steps leading up to the close are pretty consistent across the board. In this chapter, we will discuss those steps and what to expect when you are ready to buy the property

Step 1 Escrow

Escrow is the process of opening an account with a third party who will act on behalf of the two participants in the transaction. In most cases, this will be the actual property owner and the buyer. When you are purchasing real estate, there are many things that have to happen before the sale is completed and escrow is the way to protect your interests so that you are not scammed. A neutral party holds onto all the money until all the documents, title searches, and other details of the transaction are completed, and the deal has met all the requirements.

Step 2 Title Search

A title search is a crucial part of the purchase process. It gives you peace of mind and assurance that once you've made the purchase, no one can come along later and claim their right to the property. With a title search, an officer will investigate to make sure that all ties to the property are accounted for. Any third-party claims to the property are validated. If they find any, the property owner must clear these up before you take ownership of the property.

The officer who performs the search can either be from a title company or an attorney and will work to protect the buyer's interests. They will look through public records and any legal documents to identify who the true owners of the property really are. They will also look for liens or court judgments on the property and if there are any back taxes due.

It is possible to do this kind of search on your own, but it is not always easy to do. Legal documents may be difficult to understand and even knowing what records to look for is not always easy to determine. Without an experienced eye to find hidden documents you may overlook something important and once you take ownership of the property, be stuck with an additional expense that could hurt your chances to get a return on your investment.

If there are issues uncovered in the search, they will be given to you in a preliminary title report. You can then take this to the seller and ask them to resolve the issue or decide if you are willing to go through with the purchase of the property. While all issues discovered in this process are not major, some can be pretty significant and could have the potential of derailing your entire deal, so it is a good idea to include your real estate agent and/or your attorney in this process to make sure that all of your interests are protected.

Step 3 Find an Attorney

You may not feel it is necessary to get an attorney to oversee your property purchase but since you are making this a business it is definitely advisable, especially during the closing phase. The documents related to real estate purchases are often confusing and even some professionals in business have trouble understanding all the details of closing documents. Hiring an experienced real estate attorney will help you to not only get a better understanding but can zero in on problems that you might not recognize. It may cost you a little extra, but it would be money well spent.

There are many benefits to having a realtor involved in your real estate purchase, even if it will add a few thousand additional dollars to the total cost.

- They can ensure that you get the details of the agreement properly detailed in the contract.
- They can handle any liens or other issues that may come up in a title search.
- They can handle the complexities of property transfers.
- They can file all legal documents required at the county and state level.
- They can decipher the complexities of state regulations, so you are always within the confines of the law.

Without an attorney to help you with these things, your risk level increases. Aside from being caught with having to pay back taxes or liens on the property, you may also find yourself being sued for one reason or another.

Buying real estate is a very complex process and if certain aspects of the transaction are not done correctly, you could be faced with additional taxes, denial of permits, or find you are unable to get your taxpayer identification number issued among other things.

While you may cringe at the bill a real estate lawyer will send, it is worth it when you think of how much more it will cost if you miss something by doing all of this on your own.

Step 4 Get Pre-Approved for a Mortgage

Some people make this their first step so that they know exactly how much money they have to purchase a home. While it is not required, it does go a long way in proving that you have financial backing when negotiating a deal. It will give you more bargaining power and can enable you lock in your rates. Consequently, you can get some of the best interest rates possible. This outcome is important since interest rates are constantly fluctuating and can change while you're in the process of negotiations.

Step 5 Negotiate Closing Costs

The escrow company will naturally charge a fee for its services. Closing costs can vary from one company to the next. Some companies will give you a standard fee, but will up the ante by charging additional fees that you may not be aware of. While there are no set guidelines on what an escrow company can charge, much of it can be negotiated and sometimes eliminated altogether. They may charge you for additional services that may not be necessary including, for example, administrative fees, ancillary fees, application review fees, appraisal reviews, settlement fees, email fees, processing fees, etc. Do some comparison shopping to make sure they are not adding on unnecessary charges or inflating those that are legitimate.

Step 6 Home Inspection

A property inspection is not necessary but considering all the things that could go wrong with properties, it is a wise idea. Many serious problems may not be visible to the naked eye so when you go through a walkthrough, you won't notice things like plumbing, electrical, or foundation problems. Having a property inspection allows you to identify these problems before the sale is completed giving you the option to back out of the deal or demand they be fixed before you take ownership of the property.

Of course, everything found in an inspection is not going to destroy the deal but there are some things that could be big enough to become real deal breakers. A damaged foundation is one example. The cost of this type of repair could significantly impact how much money you have left over for other things. As a result, you may not be able to get a decent return on your investment.

Step 7 Pest Inspection

Like the property inspection, pest inspections are a protection for you. Having an expert come in and determine if you have any unwanted guests living in the walls that could do significant damage in the future could be a lifesaver. Even a small infestation of termites can quickly spread and cause major destruction to an expensive piece of property. If a pest problem is found, you can demand that it be taken care of before you take possession of the property.

Step 8 Renegotiate

After the inspections have been completed, you can start renegotiating your offer. Even if your initial offer has already been accepted, these can be changed if the inspections have brought out any problems. You can renegotiate the purchase price less any cost of repairs or services that may be needed or you can demand that the seller pays for these services before you take possession. However, if the seller has posted the property "as is" then there is not much room for renegotiations. It will likely be the case if you're purchasing a property to flip or to rehab. Still, you do have the freedom to pull out of the deal without penalty if the inspections reveal major problems that can't be fixed.

Negotiations are an ongoing process. It cannot be an all or nothing arrangement and there is a very definite art to it. You might think that going in hard is the way to go but a real negotiator will be willing to give a little so that both parties will win.

Before you start negotiating, give some thought to your ideal outcome from the deal. It might even be best to write down what you would consider your preferred result. It helps to be optimistic, but you should also be realistic. This situation is why the inspections are so important to do before you reach this stage.

Once you know what your preferred outcome is, then think about what you would be willing to concede, a backup position that you could live with and still close the deal. Think of as many possibilities as possible.

Then take a look at the seller's position and try to identify any potential weaknesses. Perhaps he needs to sell fast to avoid foreclosure, or he has to relocate to another part of the country. He has another property he wants to buy. Being able to identify the weaknesses is key to a good negotiation strategy.

During the negotiation, make sure you outline what you hope to get. That way the seller knows exactly how far you are from making an agreement. Then it becomes a back and forth exchange where one concedes and then the other until you reach a middle ground. Think about ways to sell your position to the other party. Why your deal works to their advantage. These could give you points that will help your cause and give you some common ground.

If you cannot come to an agreement, don't close the door entirely. Always leave so that there is a possibility of future negotiations if the other party decides to reconsider. Never burn your bridges.

Step 9 Lock in the Interest Rate

Locking in your interest rate protects you from an unexpected hike while the property is still in escrow. If you're working with a financial institution for your mortgage, they should tell you when interest rates drop so you can lock them in. You can also do this yourself by watching them online. Interest rates can be very unpredictable and can change several times a day so you will find yourself glued to your computer screen, trying to find the lowest rate possible. It is better to wait for the interest rate you feel most comfortable with and lock that in. Whether you can lock in a rate at a certain point will depend on your current credit score, your location, and the type of loan you're applying for so even with all that research you may not get the lowest possible rate available. Still, you can probably do better than just taking the first rate offered to you.

Aside from the purchase price of the home, your interest rate will be the most expensive part of real estate investing. It is crucial that you get a rate that you can work with. These rates will determine what your mortgage payments will be for the next 30 or 40 years. It helps to understand how they will affect you. The best rates are offered to those who are most creditworthy.

Below is an example of how your credit score can affect just how much your mortgage payments will be based on a $300,000 purchase on a 30-year loan.

FICO Score   Annual Percentage Rate   Monthly Payment   Interest paid

760-850	4.117	1,453
	236,937	
700-759	4.339	1,491
	236,937	
680-699	4.516	1,523
	$248,247	
660-679	4.73	1,561
	268,078	
640-659	5.16	1,640
	290,374	
620-639	5.706	1,742
	327,243	

It is easy to see how your credit score can have a major impact on just how much money you will have to pay to get ownership of that property. But other things can also affect your interest rate.

- Steady income and employment history
- Your Debt to Income Ratio
- Your down payment

Shopping around for the best interest rate and being able to lock it in is just as important as the time it takes for you to find that perfect property you want to invest in.

Step 10 - Deal with Contingencies

When you make a purchase offer, there should be several contingencies that need to be addressed. These could include anything that must be completed before the sale is closed. Some examples of contingencies could be.

1. Acquiring financing at an interest rate that does not exceed a set percentage rate
2. A successful home inspection that does not uncover major problems
3. The seller disclosing any hidden problems

4. No major infestations revealed in the pest inspection
5. All repairs completed as previously agreed to in the initial offer

Whatever the contingencies are, they must all be addressed before the deal can be closed. As each contingency is met, make sure that they are completed, recorded in writing, and dated.

Step 11 Fund Escrow

When you first signed the purchase agreement, you made a deposit to show the seller that you were serious about your desire to buy the property. For that reason, the seller took the property off the market and ceased looking for buyers. If you change your mind without good reason, the deposit you made goes to the seller for compensation for his time. If the seller does not follow through on the deal, the deposit money reverts back to you.

Now, though, you need to deposit additional funds into your escrow account. The initial deposit you made is applied to your down payment on the purchase. You now have to put in the remaining portion of the down payment and the closing costs you agreed to.

Step 12 Final Walkthrough

You have one last chance to walk through the property before signing your closing documents. You can then look for any additional damages that may have occurred since you started the agreement or to check that nothing that you're paying for has been removed from the property.

Step 13 Sign the Papers

The final stage of the purchasing process is signing the papers. It is probably one of the most important steps in the whole process. The contract will likely be 100+ pages in length. You will have others there prompting you to sign this page and that page; to initial this clause and that clause, etc. Don't let them rush you. Make sure that you understand everything on each page as well as the fine print. A real estate lawyer will be invaluable in this situation to ensure that you thoroughly understand every aspect of the document.

Check to make sure the interest rate you agreed to is correct and avoid any clause that provides for a prepayment penalty. Compare closing costs to the estimate that you were given when you first started the process. It should not vary by any more than 10%.

Purchasing real estate can be taxing and there are a myriad details that must be addressed. For the new investor, it can be quite overwhelming. Moreover, the most difficult part of the process may just be the waiting. From start to finish, you will be waiting for someone else to do their part of the transaction. You'll be waiting for papers to be signed; for mortgages to be approved; for inspections to be completed; for this work to be done and so on. So, prepare yourself ahead of time so that you don't lose your patience or get frustrated. Find something keep yourself occupied while you wait for the completion of the entire process.

Remember, acquiring the property is on the first step in your business venture. You don't want to waste all of your energy on this initial phase because there's a lot more work ahead of you.

Chapter 6: Should I Rehab?

There is something romantic about buying an old, broken down piece of property and breathing new life into it. It is the kind of project that speaks to the heart of most of us. But when the excitement dies down and it's time to actually get started with the grunt work, that rosy picture in your mind tends to lose some of its brightness.

Before you decide to do a full rehab on a property, you need to know what you are in for. There is definitely money in this type of venture, so the question really comes down to whether or not you're made for this type of business.

Consider the Costs

One of the first things you have to do is take the time to do the math. It's not always easy to figure out what you can pay for an actual fixer-upper. However, you need to have a pretty reasonable estimate as to what it will cost to completely renovate the property from its present condition. When making this estimate it is better to estimate on the higher side to cover for any additional expenses that may come up later. You may have to get a few experts to give you an honest appraisal of what the costs will be. Doing so will place you in a better position to make the judgments yourself. Note that as a beginning investor, it will definitely be worth it to pay an expert to come in and weigh in on the job.

In most cases, if the project needs a lot of extensive structural improvements it might be best to walk away from it altogether. Major repairs like complete replumbing and electrical overhauls, foundation upgrades, and extensive roof work are essential but would rarely increase the value of the property.

Once you've obtained a pretty good idea of what it will cost to totally rehab the property, your next step is to determine what the projected market value of the property would be. Choose to rehab only those projects where you can see a clear financial advantage. The ideal properties for rehabs are those that only require a face-lift so they are more aesthetically appealing. Simple touchups like painting, drywall repairs, and refinishing the floors are your best options. The cost of such repairs will be far less than structural revamping.

There are some projects where the work needed will not fit into either the structural repair aspect or the cosmetic work needed. These could be room additions, landscaping, or anything else that would bring the property up to a level where it can be competitively priced with other properties in the same neighborhood.

It can be tempting to decide to add on and do a lot more work than necessary. If you do too much, the house might come out overpriced for its community. Then you won't be able to profit from it when you're done. Ideally, improvements should not raise the value of the property more than 15% over the median price of other properties in the community.

While there is a real good chance that the property is priced well below market value, always expect that there will be unexpected expenses that will come up later. No matter how much you look and inspect, when dealing with older buildings, you will get surprises. Renovations can be very expensive. If you won't have a lot of money left over after the project, it may not be worth it for you to start this venture. Remember aside from the sale price of the property, you will also be faced with closing costs, attorney fees, and other expenses associated with the purchase. Make sure that you have enough money to cover the full expense of the rehab before you decide to buy.

Time

Finding a contractor to do the work for you can ensure that the project is done correctly and completed within a reasonable time frame. However, it is always best if you are able to pitch in. Being able to pitch in can help you to save a great deal of cash on the overall project. It takes a certain type of person to want to invest in a rehab project. These are die-hard do-it-yourselfers. It's not always about saving the money, they are hands-on people who are willing to dedicate a significant amount of time to do this type of project. If you're not that type of person and aren't willing to roll up your sleeves and put in some physical labor, then rehabbing is probably not the best way to go.

Patience is an essential quality to have. Depending on the size of the project, these types of investments can take anywhere from a month to more than a year before completion. During that entire time, you will be paying for a project that is not going to be bringing in any money. It may disrupt your personal life and have an impact on your family dynamics. If this is going to affect you negatively then rehabbing is not for you.

Money

Of course, the biggest concern you have is the money. You will have at least two major expenses. First, the expense of purchasing the property and second the cost of renovation, both of which could be quite sizeable. Majority of people do not have a lot of extra cash left over after a down payment. You have to make sure you have funds available, so you can see your way to the end of the project.

If there is not a lot of work, many people will simply use their credit card to fund the project. On the other hand, this may not be the best decision if there will be extensive work involved. Interest rates are extremely, and the expenses are not tax deductible. However, there are no up-front expenses that you will have to shell out.

Others may choose to borrow against their 401(k) or other retirement plans. Life insurance can also be a means of paying for the rehab work. In either case, these avenues of revenue do not require you to have a credit check and the interest rates generally are pretty low. It might be worth taking the initiative to investigate.

If there is to be more extensive work done, you might want to consider getting a renovation loan. These can be obtained through a home equity line of credit or it could be a part of your mortgage. With a home equity loan, you can usually borrow up to 90% of the home's value of the property after the renovations are completed. Interest rates on these types of loans are comparable with the interest rates on mortgages, but keep in mind that it will not all be tax deductible. Only about $100,000 in interest can be declared, so it pays to know how much the project will cost you before you decide on this type of loan.

There are many ways to get the money to pay for your rehab so before you decide to take the step, make sure you have financing securely in place before you begin the work.

Practicality

It is important to consider the practicality of a rehab project. There are other factors besides money that could cause a project to go bad. It's not just about bringing a building back to its original glory. It also has to fit in with the community well and appealing to renters or homebuyers when you are finished.

You have to think about the neighborhood where the property is located. Aside from checking to see what the average prices are for the area, look for the location of the schools. Take a walk around the neighborhood to see the condition of the other homes in the area. Are they being well-maintained, will your home stand out against a backdrop of old, run-down buildings? To get the property with the best potential look for these guidelines:

- **Look for the worst house on the best block.** When shopping for a new property scout out the location first. If you get a property in a location where all the buildings need work, it won't pay off in the end. It wouldn't be practical to invest in one area where the property values of the surrounding area will affect your property. Even if your finished product looks like a jewel, buyers or renters might not want to cough up the extra dough. If you purchase a property that is in need of repair in an otherwise well-manicured neighborhood, you'll not only get the support of the surrounding community, but buyers will feel as if they are getting their money's worth for the price you're asking.

- **Look for the best return on your investment.** The ideal fixer-upper is the one that looks bad but has pretty good bones. If you choose to buy a 100-year-old house, for example, but inside it has upgraded plumbing, a modern furnace and an up to code electrical system, then you can be pretty sure that you're going to get a nice return on your investment. Buyers tend to want the traditional look, but they always want the most modern conveniences. Projects that require simple upgrades, like new doors, a fresh coat of paint, and structurally sound usually good investments.

- **Think of an alternative use for the property.** It is inevitable that you will one day have a project that won't deliver on its expectations. If for example, you plan to fix up the property and then resell it but after a set period of time you've received no offers, then you have to find alternative ways for the property to make money. Perhaps you can use it as a vacation rental, or a long-term rental until the market turns around. Everything always looks pretty good on paper but there is no way to control what the market will eventually do. As long as you have an alternative way to generate money from the project, then it may be worth your time and money to proceed.

When you evaluate the condition of the property, determine whether or not you're going to be involved in a major renovation or a cosmetic upgrade. The answer will vary from one property to the next. Some of the most exciting projects are those that require an entire gut job. Putting thrills aside, you have to look at what the overall project will entail in terms of cost and time.

Factors to look at when evaluating the condition of the property are the foundations, roof, lighting, floor plan, construction, and design. In many cases, it may be difficult to put your personal opinions aside and look at the property in terms of what the buyer will want to see.

Examine the layout of the property. Many older buildings are full of walls that give a closed in feeling. See if it is possible to knock out some of those walls to bring a more open layout. If you can alter the floor plan in a way that is more up to date and modern, you'll attract more buyers. Make sure you allot money for that kind of renovation.

Finally look at the configuration of the property. Know the square footage and the number of bedrooms. If the bedrooms are small, you might want to knock out a wall and combine two to make them larger. You might think adding a room will raise the cost considerably. Such a decision, while appealing, may not be worth the investment you plan to put into it.

Decide if you are ready to take on a minor project or a major one. Minor projects will involve very basic upgrades:

- Adding a deck
- Painting the exterior
- Replacing doors
- Refinishing kitchen cabinets
- Replacing broken windows
- Installing new light fixtures
- Installing new carpet
- Refinishing floors
- Painting or wallpapering interior walls

Major work will be more extensive:

- Replacing the HVAC system or central air
- Additions like an extra room or garage
- Repairing foundations
- Remodeling the kitchen or bath
- Replacing the roof
- Replacing windows
- Installing new plumbing, electrical wiring, or sewer lines

Whenever you are deciding on taking on a rehab project, there is a lot to think about. You not only have to look at the property you're considering but you have to be able to see just how your vision will fit into the surrounding community. It is also important to have your finger on the pulse of the market. You may have a great idea and a great vision, but you are not planning this for yourself. Instead, you are planning this for a profitable venture, so you need to know if you can deliver a product that the public is willing to pay for.

Finding a Contractor

Unless you're a skilled carpenter, electrician, plumber, painter, and overall artisan, you're going to have to hire a contractor for your project. A good contractor will be able to take an ugly building, no matter what its condition, and turn it into a gem that is ready to go on the market.

Unfortunately, horror stories about contractors doing shady work, not showing up for jobs, or charging excessive prices for unbelievable delays at every turn. There is definitely a skill to cutting through all the riff-raff out there and finding a contractor that will give you quality work at an honest price.

Where to Look

One of the first things you need to know is where to look for a good contractor. Here are a few options:

- REIC: REIC stands for Real Estate Investment Club. These are investors that meet together as a group, who have already worked with contractors and can give you referrals. These are pretty reliable referrals because the contractors have a proven track record and those investors who have worked with them will vouch for their reputation.

- You can also scout around the neighborhood and look for contractors that are already on jobs nearby. When you find one, don't hesitate to stop and talk to them. Ask to see what they are working on and get a feel for how they manage their projects. If possible, talk to the person they are working for and get a feel for if they are satisfied with the job so far.

- Contractors are frequently making visits to hardware stores to get supplies. Larger chains like *Home Depot* or *Lowes* often have diligent workers that might be there in between jobs. You can usually find these contractors because they are buying a significant amount of supplies for various projects they may be working on.

- An online search can also give you a long list of possible contractors. You must be careful with these though, not all contractors listed are honest or reputable. However, if you don't have good solid referrals from trustworthy people, this is a pretty good route to take. You will have to screen them, though, to make sure that they are who they say they are. Just because they have a website doesn't mean that they are legitimate, licensed contractors. Ask for references and proof that they are qualified to do the work you want to have done. Always check their references to make sure that they have done the work they say they have and ask to see the finished project.

Follow the Rule of 3s: When you first start out working with contractors you're on unsure footing. You don't really know what to expect, what is reasonable, or what to ask for. However, if you apply the rule of 3, where you can get three different contractors to submit bids, you will have a pretty good idea of what a job will cost. Through the course of the conversations you have, you will learn a lot about what the job entails.

For example, there are the square foot formulas that they use to calculate the cost of a project. There are videos that will help you to appraise different properties and the different kinds of materials that work best for the job you have. You may not know much in the beginning, but you will learn more as you ask questions or as they ask questions of you. When you talk to several different contractors, you will gain quite an education.

Do You Need a Subcontractor?

There are different types of contractors. A general contractor will oversee all the aspects of a job, this way you don't have to be present for every phase of the project. Your other option is to hire a series of subcontractors to handle each job as it is needed. With subcontractors, it becomes your responsibility to manage and oversee every phase of a project. If you're trying to cut costs, then subcontracting will be the way to go, but if you have a regular job or other obligations that will consume a large amount of your time, it may be best to pay a general contractor to handle the full scope of the project. You can still get your hands dirty when you want, but leaving it in the hands of a good and reliable contractor can give you true peace of mind and the assurance that the job is getting done right.

No matter what the scope of your project, your contractor will be one of the most important elements in getting the job done and in a timely fashion. Your goal is to acquire the house, rehab it, and turn it over in the as short amount of time as possible. So, even if you have the skills and the qualifications to do the kind of work needed, ask yourself if you are really prepared for that type of commitment. Remember, if you are turning this into a business, your attention might be better spent elsewhere, and a contractor can help to make sure that your job is done the right way with a few delays and setbacks as possible.

Ugly is Beautiful

While everyone loves experiencing a beautiful home, the rehabber has to have an internal appreciation for the ugly. As a rehabber, you are going to be shopping for homes that other people don't want to see. You're looking for the eyesore in the neighborhood, those properties that other homeowners shake their head at and mourn the loss of their own property values because of them. You have to look past the ugly, study the bones of the structure, and have a vision of what it can become.

In such cases, the uglier the house, chances are the more profit you can make from it. That is, if you can follow through with a plan to get the job done. While you want to find ugly, never underestimate the hidden costs of a property. But once you find your first hidden treasure of ugliness, you'll be seeing a pretty balance in your bank account.

Remember, it is not just about the money. While that is what we're all in this business for, you also have to consider if you're the kind of person that can see such a project all the way to the end. Rehabbers are die-hard crafters and love to get their hands dirty. If you can get involved in such a project and you get the kind of satisfaction from that kind of work, it fits in with the whole scheme of things and it is within your budget, then it's a good bet that it is a rehab project waiting for you.

Chapter 7: Managing the Property

If you are planning to flip the house and sell it after the rehab, the next step will be to find a realtor and get the newly refurbished home out on the market. The sooner you do this, the faster you'll be able to get a return on your investment. However, if the market takes a slump and you can't find a buyer within a reasonable amount of time or you choose not to sell as you set up your own personal real estate empire. If either of these is the case, your next step is to turn your property into a rental.

Investing in rentals is a great way to build up a steady flow of cash that will cover all the expenses you still have hanging over your head after the project has completed. Many people refer to rentals as truly passive income, but that is not always the case. If your decision is to manage the property yourself, then you will be working quite a bit in order to maintain the property, deal with maintenance issues, and collecting rents.

If you are new to the rehab game, you'll start out managing the task yourself. But if you plan on buying more properties you'll have a decision to make. Should you hire a property manager or should you continue to do the work yourself? The decision is a personal one, but it starts with taking a look at yourself in the mirror.

Should You Hire a Manager?

There is a lot of work involved in managing rentals. It is not just about collecting rents and cleaning up after a tenant moves out. In addition to maintaining the property, there is a lot of paperwork involved. You'll have to file tax reports, hire workers, manage collections, interact with the tenants, deal with complaints, and several other things here and there.

You need to be sure that you are the kind of person that can actually do this kind of work. If you are going to do the work yourself, it will be a real job that you will have to report to on a regular basis, especially if you plan on having more than one property. You will have to be quick on managing problems, tough enough not to buy into tenant's sad stories, and fearless enough not to back down when problems arise.

This may be easy to do for the first few properties but after a while, it will consume all of your time and energy. Management companies are skilled at this kind of impersonal work. They are much better at screening tenants, getting them to pay on time, and already have a team of workers who will be ready to address any maintenance issues quickly.

You cannot underestimate the value of a management company for your business. They know how to screen tenants, you'll have more reliable tenants living on your property who will be paying their rent on time. They are better able to handle maintenance issues in a timely manner. You won't have to worry about your property getting run down and losing its value. Since they know how to handle complaints efficiently, you are more likely to have tenants who are happy and won't be looking to move to another location.

You also have to consider the type of properties you are invested in. If your properties all consist of single-family homes then your management skills may be sufficient. However, if you've invested in commercial properties or multi-family dwellings then being a hands-on manager may turn out to be too time-consuming for you. Let's look at all the aspects of management that you will have to deal with.

Property Evaluation

Managers can evaluate the property after a tenant vacates. You will need to walk through the property to assess what is still in working order, what may need repair, or what work needs to be done before the next tenant moves in. A property management company will have their own workers to do this for you and will usually give you a pretty reliable estimate on costs.

Rent Figures

Managers can help decide on how much rent to charge. You may believe that your rents are reasonable, but a property manager is more in tune with what the market will bear. However, you can still maintain control over this area as a property manager's goal is to rent the units fast and may not be willing to wait for a reasonable price. (They don't get paid for vacancies.)

Screening Tenants

A manager must screen the tenants and select the best one. Screening can present quite a few headaches. This involves placing ads for the property, showing it, checking references, preparing leases, doing credit checks, and collecting money. They are less emotional about the task and will not accept a tenant purely on the money they have in hand. They will select the best tenants of all the applicants because they want to make sure that the tenant will stay and pay.

Collecting Rent

Property manages will make sure that the rents are collected on time. They will not hesitate to charge late fees or let the rent slide. This sets a bad precedent and the tenants will eventually not make paying their rent a priority and may even stop paying completely. If they fall too far behind, managers will start the eviction process.

Handling Evictions

No one likes the idea of an eviction. It is never pleasant but at times it is necessary. The manager will work to get the tenant out on good terms as much as possible. If they cannot, they will take on this unpleasant task without hesitation. This will likely cost you more money but not nearly as much as having a deadbeat tenant on your hands.

Check on the Property's Condition

Managers will perform periodic checks on the property to ensure that it is being taken care of properly. In many leases, there is a clause that has been included allowing for an annual or bi-annual check to ensure that the property is being maintained properly. Property managers will notify tenants and do the inspection to make sure the house is not being damaged in any way.

Thorough Inspection

Managers can have properties thoroughly inspected before they are rented. Even after rental, expect that things will break and must be fixed. Regular maintenance before, during, and after a tenant moves in is their responsibility. They are available 24/7 to make sure that these problems are addressed for the benefit of both you and the tenant.

Paperwork

Managers also handle all of the necessary paperwork associated with the property. These include accounting and taxes. They will keep track of how much rent you've collected, how much maintenance costs you, manage your profit/losses and supply you with a year-end report.

You may choose to start out managing the property yourself, but as your business grows, you are likely going to be much more interested in hiring a property manager to handle much of the grunt work for you.

Paying Your Property Manager

Managing properties is not an easy job. There are a lot of small details that need to be taken care of. This doesn't mean that all properties will be equally hard to manage. Not all the tenants will pay their rent late, the same way, not every unit will require a steady flow of repairs, and issues are not going to come up in every case. In fact, there are properties that will be successfully rented out for years without ever having a problem.

So, how much should you expect to pay your property manager? In short, every case is going to be different. Many people feel that hiring a manager may not be worth it, or they've had bad experiences with ineffective managers in the past. As the owner of the property, the tenant should recognize that you make all the decisions, which can make it hard for you if a problem comes up. Most people want managers to handle complicated situations like evictions, screening, and handling complaints. If you don't mind dealing with these possible problems, you may not have to worry about hiring a manager.

However, you don't want to wait until you have a problem to hire a manager. If you do decide to hire one, it means you can expect to pay a percentage of your rents collected every month to cover their fees, which usually range from 8 to 12% every month. From that, some management companies may have additional fees. It is worth negotiating exactly what you want them to do and how much you are willing to pay for it.

Investment of Time

Your decision to hire a manager will depend a great deal on how much work is involved. Managing a lot of properties will naturally take a lot of time. However, if you only have one property, it may not be worth it for you to hire someone. It may only take an investment of a few hours every month to go over, cut the grass, or take care of the regular maintenance duties, collect the rents, and make bank deposits.

The need comes up when you have multiple rental properties to manage. A few hours per month now increases to a few hours per week or more. Managing multiple problems might result in things getting out of hand very quickly. If you do not have the time to deal with them, then it's quite clear that best thing for you to do is hire a manager.

If you think you can handle the extra workload, there are several strategies that can help you to keep on top of things. You need to be organized, with a system that schedules when you need to collect your rent and keep a record of who paid. When you are dealing with multiple properties, this can seem like a breeze at first, but in time, other priorities might be put first. When that happens, if you want to keep your business solvent, seriously consider hiring a manager.

Renting Out Your Property

For onlookers, renting out a property seems pretty easy. Set a price, place an ad, and get a tenant, collect the rent and you're done. Well, that's the basics but there is a lot more involved than that. Let's go through the steps on how to rent out your property in the most efficient manner

First, determine how much rent you can reasonably expect for your property. This can be a tricky process because the amount of rent is not determined just by the value of the house but also by what the market can stand. In most areas in the country, how much you got for selling your property as a matter of public record, but how much you got in rent is not. The only way you can get a ballpark figure of what everyone else is paying is to study the active rental ads for vacancies in your area, or you can talk to a rental agency.

Deciding this figure should be determined even before you decide to purchase the property. It should have a bearing on how much you're willing to pay to buy and renovate if you don't reasonably expect to get that money back and some in rent, it is really not worth making the investment in the first place.

As you go through the rental listings in your area, take note of all the properties that are similar to yours and then check back periodically to see how long they took to rent out. You can usually tell when a property is rented because the ad will be removed. You can call to double check just to make sure.

A property manager knows what is a reasonable rent to ask, especially if they are responsible for managing a lot of properties. Make sure you screen your managers carefully though, some will take a shortcut and undercut your rent just so they can get money faster.

If you're still not sure how to price your rental you can get a rent report from rentrange.com, which will do the comparison work for you. Registering with them will give you a good picture of how much the rents are going for in your area and what reminders you should be aware of specifically in your area.

Pricing Your Property

Once you have the range of rentals in your area, you have to come down to a specific figure. There are several different methods investors do.

1. Some price the rents at the top range of what the market will accept, hoping to find a renter who is willing to pay for quality.
2. Others price just below the market, so they get a lot of applicants and can choose the best one.

Which strategy you choose depends on your preference. With option one, you get a renter who doesn't mind paying a little extra for a nicer home, but with option two, you know who gets your place. There are pros and cons to both methods.

Once you've determined the rent for the property, you need to place an ad. This can be anything from sticking a for rent sign in the window or posting on an online classified ad space. Before you do this, you need to learn how potential renters seek out properties in your area. Some will go to online sites like Zillow first while others will turn to ads on Craigslist, a local flyer, or through other channels. You need to be where the renters are looking otherwise, it could take months for the right tenant to find your property.

Showing the Property

Once potential renters see your ad, you now have to show the property to them. You can either have an open house where they can walk in freely or have them schedule an appointment for a walkthrough. The open house frees up a lot of your time and can possibly attract more potential renters who never saw your ad. The scheduled walkthrough gives you more one on one time with the individuals to find out what kind of tenants they may be.

When interest is shown, you can start the application process. You can find many standard rental applications online that you can adjust to your needs. You can also have your lawyer draw up one specifically designed for your unique qualifications. Most landlords charge a rental fee that will cover this expense and a credit check. A good potential tenant won't have any problem with paying the fees and it is a way to make sure that the applicant is serious about renting your property.

It is important that you observe the person as he goes through the property. Study the application carefully. The goal is to learn as much as possible about them. The more they talk, the better the picture you'll get about how they will live in your place. Their application needs to be filled out thoroughly with no blank spaces, several verifiable references, and necessary information to check their credit. Always check references, especially for their last place of residence. Find out not just if they paid their rent on time but if they were a nuisance tenant or not. Did they destroy the place or were they responsible.

Employment verification is key. If they have only been working for a short period of time, which may be a cause for concern. However, if they have been on the job a long time it is evidence of a stable income.

Pets or No Pets

The decision to rent to pet owners is a personal one. It also depends on the kind of pet. If they have a dog that loves to chew on furniture or has a very destructive nature then you will rightly be very concerned about renting to them. However, if they have a pet that is calm, friendly and won't be a threat to the neighbors, then you can make room for him in your place.

You can require an additional deposit for pets in case of damage. Pets can easily destroy carpeting, flooring, and even drywall. Some have been known to chew on doors or dig up and destroy beautifully manicured lawns.

True pet lovers won't hesitate to pay an additional deposit for their pets to have a home. They may even be willing to pay more in monthly rent just to keep their loved one with them. This can definitely make it worth your while, on the long run, to have a pet stay in your place. As a general rule, consider gauging the extra charge based on the size of the animal. The larger the animal the more damage he could do, therefore the more the tenant should have to pay.

You also need to check with your local city ordinance about the kinds of pets allowed in the community. You may be okay with a pit bull on your property, but some city ordinances have strict regulations against such breeds. If something were to happen, then you would be held liable for allowing the pet on your premises.

Some pet owners will state that their pet is a little angel. How can you know for sure? One of the best ways to find out is to talk to previous landlords to find out what the pet was like in the last home. You can also request them to bring the pet in so you can see how he interacts with others. It pays to put a clause in their lease that stipulates that if they do not comply with your regulations on pets on the premises they can be fined an additional fee for the inconvenience.

Writing the Lease

Another matter you'll have to deal with if you don't have a property manager is the lease. This can be a pretty technical job and every detail needs to be stipulated in writing. Not just the amount of rent to be paid, but charges for late fees, due dates, and what the tenants are allowed and not allowed to do.

This is important and you should not leave anything out. If you want to have a non-smoking property, it must be written that smoking is not permitted. Clauses for pets, guests, parties, painting, remodeling, parking, and any other type of activity that a tenant may end up doing should also be included. It should be stipulated clearly and there should be some form of penalty for breaking any of the clauses.

You also need to detail what your responsibilities are as the property owner and those of the manager as well. As such, if there are any disclosures about the property they must be spelled out clearly. If you have purchased an older property, there may reason to explain the dangers of lead-based paint. This applies to any property built prior to 1978. There may be other disclosures you need to stipulate as well including details about carbon monoxide and smoke detectors.

The Search for a Property Manager

After reading this chapter you may very well be thinking it would be worth it to hire a property manager. If that is the case, the next step is to find one. Just like you would carefully screen your tenants, you also must screen your manager to make sure that he will be a good fit for the job. There are several options to search for a property manager:

- Online

- Word of mouth
- Ask for references
- Get recommendations from your title company

Once you have several managers to choose from, start checking their background.

- Check their website to see how many properties they have listed
- Find out how many units they manage
- Check the vacancy rate against their numbers (If their percentages are higher than in the local area, they may not be the right manager for you)
- Call the company and pretend to be a potential renter
- Do a drive-by of their property to see how well it's been kept.
- Check with the BBB (Better Business Bureau) to see if there have been any complaints filed against them.

The Interview Process:

From the preliminary checks, you can narrow down your prospects before you speak with them face-to-face. They will likely have their own speech to give you, but you should ask your own questions as well. Here are a few ideas to get you started.

- What type of rentals do you specialize in?
- How long have you been a manager?
- Are you in good standing with the BBB?
- How large is your staff?
- Do you have a real estate license?
- What are your fees?
- What do they cover?
- Do you have any established relationships with any contractors, repair companies, or other people in the real estate business?
- Do you own your own rental properties?
- Are you insured?

These are just some simple guidelines to help you to narrow down your choices and pick the right person to manage your property. In time, you will develop your own list of questions tailored to your specific needs in a manager.

There are many variables involved in choosing a property manager. Whether you choose to go this route or not will depend on you and what you expect to get out of your rental. It is not wrong to manage the property yourself but as you grow your business, chances are your attention will become divided. When that happens don't hesitate to turn it all over to a dependable manager. You will find you can earn more money and have more free time on your hands. Your rental business really can be considered as a truly passive income!

Chapter 8: Risks and Myths

Have you ever found yourself up late at night and can't sleep by the infomercials that make real estate investing sound like a breeze? They promise that you can take $20 and turn it into a million with a simple house flip. There are countless shows on TV now that make flipping or rehabbing a house seem so easy it can be done in a quick thirty minutes.

It's true, real estate investing is one of the most reliable ways to generate income. It has been that way for generations and is not likely to change soon. There are many benefits to owning investment properties and generating a nice rental income. Still, though real estate is a pretty safe investment, it is not for everyone. It is no child's play. As more and more people recognize the possibilities, it can quickly become a highly competitive market.

Just like with any other investment plan, there are risks involved and myths that can take you down the wrong path. Much of what you learn about real estate you will pick up as you go, but there are some things you don't want to leave to chance. The cost of the lesson is just not worth it.

Risk #1: Unpredictable Market

Since the real estate downfall in 2008, the market has recovered quite well. However, it is no guarantee that the uptrend we are currently experiencing will continue. Just like many other investment instruments, the real estate market has its natural ebbs and flows and can turn at any time. Economic conditions, governmental changes, and even the political landscape can have an impact on how well your business grows in the future. So, even though the market is good today, does not mean it will continue that way when you take the plunge.

You may buy a property when the demand is high, but the tides can turn suddenly and you may not be able to sell when you are ready. For this reason, when you enter into this market, you need to proceed with caution. Always stay abreast of the dynamics, the economy, and how it functions and have a backup plan that will tide you over if things get rocky.

Risk #2: Be Location Conscious

Location is going to be very important when making all of your decisions. You may not care too much about living in a remote location. Buying property for your personal use is one thing, but if you're looking for investment property, you need to think like a consumer. The location of the property should always be a top factor when it comes to purchasing real estate. Think of all the things that location will dictate in regards to your investment:

- Supply and demand. Finding a nice place in a low-cost neighborhood will increase competition so you won't be able to get to the rental price you want.
- Crime rate: No matter how beautifully you rehab a home, if it is in a high crime area, you're going to get less than desirable tenants or you won't get a decent rent for your property.
- Property values: The location also dictates what the property values will be. If you invest in an area where there are a lot of low valued homes, your renovations may be for naught.

Choosing the right location can be one of the most important decisions you can make in the real estate investing business.

Risk #3: Negative Cash Flow

Your cash flow is the amount of profit you will earn after paying off your expenses. If you can't sell the property for what you expect or you can't rent it for the right price, you run the risk of a negative cash flow. This means that after you pay your mortgage, taxes, and all the other expenses connected to the property you can still end up owing money.

To avoid this, always do a real estate market analysis before purchasing a property. You may want to hire an accountant to help you. While it won't eliminate the risk entirely, it can certainly cut down your chances of running into this problem.

Risk #4: Vacancy Risk

For every day your property is not occupied you lose money. There is no guarantee that your home will be filled 100% of the time, but you will have to take steps to keep your vacancy rates down to a minimum. As a backup plan, make sure that you have enough cash on hand to cover your mortgage so that you don't rely entirely on your rental income to pay it. Remember, in addition to the mortgage payments, you also need to pay property taxes, insurance, maintenance, and other expenses as well.

Risk #5: Bad Tenants

Even with thorough vetting, it is possible to get a bad tenant that won't pay his rent on time or will destroy the property. When that happens you will be faced with huge and costly problems including the nasty business of evictions and repairs.

To reduce this risk, ensure that you always screen your tenants carefully, check their credit score, and verify references.

Risk #6: Hidden Property Damage

Structural damage can be very expensive to recover from. In some cases, the cost of such repairs may be well out of your reach. Whenever you buy an older property, there is always a risk of hidden structural damage. To avoid this, always get the inspections done by a reliable service to find these hidden problems before you finalize the purchase.

Risk #7: Lack of Liquidity

Your real estate property may be worth a lot of money, but you may not be able to convert that into cash if you need it right away. It is not easy to sell a house and even when you find a buyer. You may find that the process from start to finish can take months. This can mean not having access to money you need in a crunch.

Risk #8: Foreclosure

If things don't go your way for an extended period of time, you run the risk of foreclosure and you could lose everything. Losing your investment to the bank can be a very painful experience and it can make it difficult for you to acquire other properties in the future. It could spell the end of your real estate venture.

Risk #9: Depreciation

The value of your property may go down rather than up through no fault of your own. Naturally, people expect real estate values to go up, but that is not always the case. All sorts of factors could affect your property values and you could end up losing money in the process.

Risk #10: Vacation Rental Issues

It is true that the vacation rental business is booming. So much so, that local legislation has set limits to the number of properties that can exist in certain areas. They may be compelled to do this as a result of pressure from established hotels in the region or pressure from local residents. If you're planning on using your property as a vacation rental, make sure you check with the legal authorities on any restrictions you may have to deal with.

Of course, you may not be faced with all of these problems overnight, but they should be of real concern to you. As you plan your investment decisions, make sure that you have a backup plan in case you meet any of these problems. Having a strategy in place can be very effective in keeping you from losing your business altogether.

Common Myths on Real Estate Investing

Another area that new investors need to be really concerned about is the common myths and misconceptions about how the real estate industry actually works. It is easy to buy into all the hype surrounding the industry, so you might be fooled into thinking that it is all pretty easy to do. There is a lot of work involved in real estate but if you do your homework, you have a good chance of being successful, as long as you don't fall into all the myths and fairy tales that people make about real estate investing.

You Need a Lot of Cash

This is a common belief that to invest in real estate you need to have a lot of cash at your disposal. That depends on the type of transaction you decide to use. It is possible to get into real estate and make a huge profit without a dime of your own money. In fact, you do not need to have your own cash or even a good credit rating to make a deal! While it is true that having cash can seal a deal a lot easier, it is not necessary. We live in a time when there are plenty of alternative financing resources that you can go to. As long as you can create an offer that is beneficial for both parties, you can generate a lot of cash with other people's money.

You Need Specialized Knowledge

Many people enter the real estate market without any experience whatsoever. It is an industry that allows you to learn as you go. The more properties you invest in, the more knowledge you pick up. Real estate is a very complex industry with many different facets. Even if you have some knowledge in one aspect of it there is always something more you can learn. You will make mistakes from time to time but that is the case with everything.

You can start with some basic skills and continue to add to them. You may not have gone to school to learn how to invest but you've already acquired some knowledge. Perhaps your parents owned property and you learned a lot just from listening to them talk about it. You've probably read a few books (this one included) that will give you more of the basics. As you grow in this business, the specialized knowledge will grow with you. Don't let this myth hold you back from getting into this lucrative investment game.

You Need a License or Certification

There is no license required to invest in real estate. Just like there is no license required to buy and sell other assets. There are licenses required to be a realtor, or a contractor but to buy, sell, rent, rehab, or flip properties, there is no need to be an agent to do these things. If you want to use those services that require licensing, you can simply hire someone with a license to do it for you. All you need is the smarts to negotiate a good deal.

It's Financially Draining

Not if you don't let it. In any investment venture, there is always a risk of losing money, but a smart investor does his homework first and then analyzes his circumstances often those who lose their money are those who are too eager to do the grunt work and are often caught off guard. Research reduces your risk of losing your shirt in a bad investment.

There are enough people out there that will discourage you from doing what you want to do. They may tell you these myths because of their own fears or they may have a bad experience themselves. Still, don't base your decision on getting into real estate investing until you've had all the facts and seen every side of the issue. By doing a little research, you will find ways to dispel all those twisted stories and get down to the core of this business. Only then can you decide whether this type of investing is right for you.

Chapter 9: Common Mistakes for New Investors

It is obvious, that real estate investing is full of many pitfalls. The road to success is filled with twists and turns and potholes that could sink your business if you're not careful. It's reasonable to expect that you will make mistakes in the beginning. Just like with anything new you try, you will trip and stumble but as you learn the ropes you will also get your footing and eventually you'll be able to stand up balance all the many facets of this industry.

Still, it can help a lot to get a little warning about how to avoid making the common mistakes new real estate investors do. Pay close attention to the list below to avoid those mistakes and get on the fast track to a profitable income. By learning these things first, you will have less to worry about and can start earning a good profit well ahead of time.

Failing Research

Real estate is just like any other business. You need to run it professionally to be successful. It means the shooting from the hip type attitude or figuring things out as you go can only take you so far. You wouldn't expect other professions to meet your needs the same way. Imagine a doctor about to perform surgery, reading the anatomy book on the way into the operating room. No patient will trust him with anything.

For some reason, many people feel they can get away with this attitude when it comes to real estate. When you think that the purchases you plan to make with your new business are going to be the largest you will ever make in your life, it is reasonable to pause and take your time to think. You are about to put your entire financial reputation into this business, it makes sense that you will want to do some research.

It's good that you've decided to read this book, but we have only scratched the surface of this business. Continue to read, to study, to analyze every aspect of the industry. In addition, find out about the people you are working in it. Real estate is not something you can do entirely on your own. You will be overwhelmed. At the same time, you don't want to trust anyone with your most valuable assets. Research is the key to avoiding very costly mistakes. Research is essential at every phase of your investment. If you do, you lower your risk of losing your money on a poor decision simply because you didn't take the time to find out the details.

Hesitation

New investors typically have two destructive patterns. The one that jumps in without doing his due diligence and the one who hesitates too long. It's true, the real estate market can be very uncertain at times and can be very competitive to boot and it pays to proceed with caution, but you cannot hesitate to a point it paralyzes your business.

Whether you're trying to buy a property or sell it, you sitting on the sidelines far too long can cost you to miss out on great opportunities. There are many reasons why you might want to wait. You might be trying to time the market so you can get the best price for your property, you're not sure if the market is going to take a downturn, you're afraid that you don't have the right kind of backing.

All these are legitimate concerns but they can also become so ingrained in you that you fail to make any decision in a timely manner. Some even reach a point where they are so afraid of making a mistake that they get that deer in the headlights, literally frozen in place while they wait for a more opportune time.

This doesn't just happen when you're getting into a deal, it can happen at any moment throughout the deal. Some are afraid to make a decision on an agent, a contractor, an accountant, or even the price. Just about every phase of the market can be crippled by hesitation. Soon, days will slip by and you'll lose what little hold you had on your business and lose out completely.

If you're really serious about the real estate business you need to have the kind of mindset that will allow you to take risks no matter how much preparation you have. Hesitating and waiting for a perfect scenario will have you sitting on the sidelines while others pass you buy and reap your rewards.

Failing to Look at Enough Properties

You may be eager to get into the real estate business but that doesn't mean you should jump in with the first property you see. It pays to shop around. When we are new, we are often too eager to get started and there may be things that we miss out on in our search. While that first property can be very exciting, you can use what you learn from the first few properties as a springboard to push you forward on your real estate journey.

Often, we are drawn to the things that we are familiar with. If you are accustomed to single-dwelling housing, have lived in them all your life, it may be difficult in the beginning to branch out and look at different types of properties. If you're accustomed to high-rise buildings, it may seem strange to look at properties in the suburbs. Your first love in real estate will most likely be something that feels like home to you. Everything else will seem strange and awkward. But after you've searched around for a few weeks or a few months, you'll begin to develop a different perspective and start to appreciate all sorts of properties. Then you'll be able to see where certain structures are better suited for varying situations.

Through the process of searching, you'll learn about features that you never thought of, you'll learn that there are new things that appeal to you. You'll experience a lot of different properties. As a result, you'll have a broader perspective about the community and what people are actually looking for.

Don't look at viewing properties merely a means to find a property to invest in. View it as a learning opportunity and an experience that will teach you everything you need to know about the area and what people want.

Getting Too Emotionally Involved

In most career choices, getting emotionally involved can be an advantage but that is not the case with real estate. It is important to have some level of passion for what you are doing, but you should be equally as passionate about maintaining your bottom line.

You might see a property that is everything you ever dreamed of, but if the numbers don't add up, it is not a good investment. Getting too emotionally attached to properties can cause you to act without reason, which could lead you down a path to financial ruin. You may end up spending too much money buying a property with no hope of ever earning it back. You might spend too much in rehabbing without any means of recouping your expenses.

It is okay to get excited about a good property when you find it, but that enthusiasm should be tempered with financial support. After all, that is what you are in business for. So, the next time you get overly excited about a property, take a pause and try to analyze why you are excited. If you see it as a good investment opportunity then it may be an opportunity just waiting for you. However, if you are excited because it makes you nostalgic for the good old days, or it looked just like a place you once saw in a magazine, then you might be getting too emotionally involved and you need to readjust your thinking.

If you find that the property doesn't meet up with your financial expectations, it probably won't meet the expectations of other investors either. You might still be on the market months later. Keep a watch on it, and in time you might see a price drop or it may work better for you at a different time.

Anytime you find yourself getting too emotionally involved in a property, it is always good to have someone there to remind you of why you got into the business in the first place. For most, it is to build a solid financial future and a business that will generate income that you can rely on.

Real Estate is a Get Rich Quick Scheme

As much as you may want it to, real estate investing is not the way to get rich overnight. No matter what you may have heard, it takes time to build up a real estate business. Just buying one property can take months to finalize. You have to put in a lot of hard work, research, and time in order to get the best return on your investment.

Buying into the hype on television will just have you more discouraged. While it is a great way to make lots of money, it will take a major commitment on your part. The good news is that if you work hard and don't give up, there is a good chance that you can have a niche that will be very profitable for you in the future.

Ignoring the Fine Print

Often, when that contract is sitting in front of you, you feel a strong push to sign it without reading and understanding everything. It is a common problem that exists in other areas besides real estate. The documents can be quite extensive, sometimes as much as a hundred pages.

It seems that these documents have been specifically worded to put you in a catatonic state. However, buying real estate is a very serious business and the consequences of not reading the fine print could be disastrous!

Often there are clauses that work to the benefit of the seller, or you may find that you are agreeing to some action you would never have considered doing otherwise.

It's important to know everything that is expected of you and the other party.

In real estate, you're going to be signing a lot of contracts and you need to prepare for those really long ones that may have hidden clauses. Do not be careless with your contracts.

Here are some tips to look into for mortgage agreements:

- In mortgage agreements, look out for those provisions, that restrict or eliminate your right to pursue matters in court.
- Mortgage companies also reserve the right to sell your personal information, so look for places in the contract that tell where your personal data is going.
- Check the main sections to be sure that the agreement matches your own understanding of what you're buying.
- Look for details on the property taxes and insurance requirements. As your loan matures

these are factors that will not stay the same. The cost may go up or down based on what you do with the property.
- If at all possible, ask for the contract ahead of the signing date so that you can read it at your leisure without the realtor, seller, and other anxious people hovering over your shoulder.

Another contract you will sign a lot of is your lease agreement.

- Make sure the verbiage states clearly what will happen to security deposits
- The due date for rent is clearly stipulated
- That you have a clear right to enter the property for inspections
- Rules about quiet hours, smoking, and overnight guests are clearly laid out
- And what to do in case of a dispute

- Other things you can think about adding are lease termination fees, late fees, and the tenant's requirement to maintain the property.

Regardless of your goals in this new venture, as a new investor, the first thing you must learn is to do your due diligence in every aspect of every transaction. You are less likely to make mistakes and end up with a profitable outcome. No deal will match your expectations exactly and you will make mistakes along the way. However, if you keep the basics in mind, avoid the common pitfalls listed here and set up processes to keep you moving straight ahead, you'll put yourself in a position where you will have a better chance at success than failure.

Conclusion

Thanks for making it through to the end of *Real Estate Investing*! We hope it was informative and it provided you with all of the tools you need to achieve your goals whatever it may be.

Investing in real estate has proven to be a lucrative way to generate a steady flow of income for many. However, it is important that you ease into this industry until you get a feel for it. While all aspects of the industry can be quite worthwhile, newbies might want to start by getting their feet wet with a small residential property to flip and then rent out. You'll end up with a regular flow of cash coming your way, which can infuse you with more enthusiasm. After you've tasted the money, it will be easy to move on to more adventurous projects.

If you invest wisely, rental properties and flips can literally change your whole perspective on the business. Move to commercial properties as a more lucrative way to make money.

Of course, these are merely suggestions. Each investor has to find the right niche for them. But, the bottom line is that there is a lot of money in real estate investing! It is waiting for you to take advantage of it.

In this book, we've touched on many subjects and I encourage you to continue growing your knowledge from here. From this book you've learned:

- How much you can make
- How to get started in real estate
- Where to look for the best deals
- The steps to buying property
- How to analyze if rehabbing and flipping are right for you
- How to determine if you need to hire extra help to manage your business
- And much more

www.ingramcontent.com/pod-product-compliance
Ingram Content Group UK Ltd.
Pitfield, Milton Keynes, MK11 3LW, UK
UKHW022227230426
12048UKWH00016BA/1103